CLASSIC NEEDLEWORK

Woven coverlet in the Single Snowball pattern, nineteenth century. (Author's collection. Photo by Ken Kaplowitz.)

CLASSIC NEEDLEWORK:
Contemporary Designs Inspired by the American Past

JUDITH GROW

with photographs by Kenneth Kaplowitz

VNR VAN NOSTRAND REINHOLD COMPANY
New York Cincinnati Toronto London Melbourne

This book is dedicated to my mother, whose talent with a needle has always been my greatest inspiration.

Printed in the United States of America
Designed by Loudan Enterprises

Published in 1976 by Van Nostrand Reinhold Company
A Division of Litton Educational Publishing, Inc.
450 West 33rd Street
New York, NY 10001

Van Nostrand Reinhold Limited
1410 Birchmount Road
Scarborough, Ontario M1P 2E7, Canada

Van Nostrand Reinhold Australia Pty. Ltd.
17 Queen Street
Mitcham, Victoria 3132, Australia

Van Nostrand Reinhold Company Ltd.
Molly Millars Lane
Wokingham, Berkshire, England

16 15 14 13 12 11 10 9 8 7 6 5 4 3 2 1

Library of Congress Cataloging in Publication Data

Grow, Judith K
    Classic needlework.

    Includes index.
    1. Needlework—Patterns. 2. Embroidery—Patterns.
I. Title.
TT753.G78   746.4   76-8681
ISBN 0-442-22881-3

Acknowledgments

Many people helped in the preparation of this book. I would like to express my special thanks to Mrs. Daniel Bailey, Mrs. Henry Halpern, Mrs. Carl Hensley, Mrs. Samuel Kaman, Mrs. Frederick Kraus, Mr. and Mrs. Richard Potts, Mrs. Dan Pullen, Mrs. Douglas Wengel, and Mrs. Dennis Wyckoff, each of whom contributed to the new projects included in the book.

My extraspecial thanks to Mrs. Robert Greiff, who from the very beginning gave her expert assistance in all phases of writing this book.

I would also like to thank the many people who helped by being generous with their time, their information, their expertise, and their precious antiques: Ms. Valerie Cunningham, Ms. Barbara Fimbel, Mr. Howell Heaney and Mr. Frank Halpern of the Free Library of Philadelphia, Mr. Thompson Harlow of the Connecticut Historical Society, Mrs. Daniel Herrick, Ms. Christina Jackson of the Philadelphia Museum of Art, Mr. Stewart Johnson of the Cooper-Hewitt Museum, Mr. Kenneth Kaplowitz, The Pink House Antiques, New Hope, Pennsylvania, Ms. Penny Pypcznski, the Queenstown Shop, Pennington, New Jersey, Carl Rist, Jr. of Interior Crafts, Chalfont, Pennsylvania, Mr. and Mrs. Richard Sudlow, Mr. and Mrs. Bruce Westcott, and Ms. Elizabeth Winton of the Old Gaol Museum, York, Maine.

Last but not least I must acknowledge the encouragement and technical help given freely by my husband, Allan, who also managed somehow to add some of my home chores to his own heavy schedule. And to Matthew and Justin, who had the difficult job of sharing Mommy with "the book," my love.

CONTENTS

Cross-stitch rug (40" × 60" excluding fringe) worked by the author and cross-stitch pillow worked by Lynda Pullen, both with a design adapted from a woven coverlet in the Whig Rose pattern. (Photo by Ken Kaplowitz.)

1. NEEDLEWORK-A LONG TRADITION

The American needleworker, armed with canvas or cloth and brightly colored strands of thread, is working in a tradition as old as the country itself. The Pilgrims, landing on New England's rocky coast, brought with them not only the basic tools necessary for founding a new land but also the decorative stitchery of the old, or at least a memory of its traditions. The earliest surviving example of American needlework is, appropriately enough, a sampler showing a variety of stitches and designs. It was worked, probably around 1635, by Loara Standish, the daughter of Miles Standish. Like other seventeenth-century samplers it is long and narrow, with examples of geometric and floral borders and of lettering. The purpose of such an "exemplar," or stitch record, was evidently to provide a reference to a repertoire of motifs for marking household linens.

By the eighteenth century the colonists had time to provide for something beyond the bare necessities of food, clothing, and shelter. Needleworkers began to ply their craft for purposes similar to those that inspire us today. Both free embroidery, such as crewel, and counted-thread embroidery, the various forms of needlepoint, were applied to pictures and decorative hangings, draperies and upholstery, rugs and coverlets, and articles of clothing ranging from slippers and purses worked in tough wools to the finest of gowns and waistcoats worked in delicate silks.

Just as we often turn to the past for inspiration, so did our eighteenth-century counterparts. The curling tendrils with flowers and animals, typical of so much early American crewelwork, were derived from English embroidery designs dating back to the days of Elizabeth I. English flowers—roses, carnations, and honeysuckles—were interspersed with birds, butterflies, and small animals. By the seventeenth century, when trade with the Far East had opened, motifs from India and China—the palmette, the tree of life, exotic birds and animals—were intermingled with the older traditional forms.

American needleworkers turned to English embroideries for ideas but never copied them slavishly. American work of the eighteenth century tends to be more open and lighter than English examples. There is an economy of design, stitches, and materials. This was probably the result of both taste and necessity. Materials in the colonies were scarce and relatively expensive. There were a few professional embroiderers in such cities as Philadelphia and Boston, but most American embroidery was worked by women who stitched useful and decorative objects for their own households with the materials at hand. The simpler forms of their work were in keeping with the design of American buildings and furnishings. Adapting traditional designs to fit their own needs, American needleworkers added to the range of motifs. The corn tassel was joined by other native plants and animals. After the Revolution the eagle, the rising sun, Liberty, and other patriotic themes were added to the repertoire. Many craftswomen, like Mary Bulman, who worked the magnificent bed hangings shown in figure 3-1, created their own designs loosely based on traditional sources. However, by the middle of the eighteenth century patterns, designs drawn on fabric, and even what we would call "kits" were available. An elaborate embroidered picture known as *The Fishing Lady and the Boston Common* appeared in several versions, all worked in the Boston area around 1745. Although the design is based on an English engraving, all the known examples portray a landscape similar to that of the Boston Common, dotted with buildings of New England character. The bed-rug design shown in figure 3-11 must have been based on a printed pattern, for numerous examples have been found throughout New England, almost all worked in the first decade of the nineteenth century. Yet it is obvious that these patterns were not followed slavishly. Elizabeth Foot, who worked the bed rug illustrated in this book, used an elaborately varied monochromatic scheme, accented with white. An example of similar design, in the Metropolitan Museum of Art, exhibits broader areas of color and employs oranges, russets, olive green, and brown. Skilled needleworkers have always adapted designs to fit their own tastes and decor, their own desire for boldness or refinement.

These personal preferences, however, have always been modified by the taste of the times and by available materials. The floral designs of the eighteenth century, with their sinuous curves and generous open intervals between motifs, were particularly congenial to free embroidery, although some counted-thread work was also done. In the nineteenth century needlepoint became overwhelmingly popular. This was partly due to the period's preference, at least after the first quarter of the century, for heavier, more robust forms and partly to

the availability of new materials.

By the end of the century patterns were available, particularly from Germany, which were marked off in graphed squares with symbols much as we know them today. By the early nineteenth century they were printed in color. From the 1830s through the 1870s these patterns were widely disseminated through the pages of such popular magazines as *Godey's Lady's Book, Frank Leslie's Illustrated Weekly, Peterson's,* and *Harper's Bazaar.* The tiger illustrated in figure 3-49 is based on such a pattern from *Godey's.* New canvases and new wools made their appearance and contributed to the popularity of needlepoint. The canvases resembled modern types in the even spacing of threads. Even a beginner could turn out a creditable piece of needlework with graphs and evenly spaced threads as guides. The industrialization of spinning and the development of aniline dyes lowered the cost of yarn. It also made available a far wider range of colors, many of them brighter and more brilliant than had ever been derived from vegetable dyes. At the same time these commercially produced yarns were somewhat coarser than those generally used in the eighteenth century. They tended to produce a larger stitch, which altered the scale and texture of nineteenth-century embroidery. As with printed patterns, Germany was the leading producer of these brilliantly colored woolens. The yarns became known as Berlin wools, and the needlepoint produced with them as Berlin woolwork.

These new materials were the product of the industrial revolution. So too was the enormous popularity of needlework. Just as today we react against the homogenized products of our society, so the Victorians experienced waves of reaction against the results of industrialization. As the urban environment grew more drab, every effort was made to decorate and brighten the interior of the home. As agricultural societies became urbanized and industrialized, women, especially in the rising middle class, had more leisure to create needlework.

Not only was more needlework done, but new subjects became popular, and needlework was applied to more objects than ever before. In the early part of the century needlework pictures, of which mourning scenes were the most popular, were frequently worked both in wool and in silk. Some highly skilled needleworkers produced elaborate copies of paintings, presumably from charts since several of these exist in more than one version. Lettering escaped from the sampler and became a decorative motif in itself in the form of Biblical quotations and patriotic mottoes, particularly popular in the 1830s and 1840s. Animals assumed a new importance. Mournful spaniels and perky terriers, fierce lions and tigers looked out from pictures, pillows, and footstools.

Still, as well as inventing new subjects needleworkers continued to look to the past for inspiration. In the mid-nineteenth century needlepoint upholstery reached a peak of popularity. A frequent design source was the floral upholsteries and tapestries of eighteenth-century France, a fitting complement to the fashionable Rococo Revival furniture. Floral and geometric motifs related to medieval tapestries were also used on Gothic-inspired chairs and sofas. Turkeywork was revived in the 1860s, and oriental motifs enjoyed a popularity they had not known since the seventeenth century and would not know again until today. But not only upholstered pieces were covered with needlework: it was applied to almost anything that could be covered. Tables, pianos, wastebaskets, desk accessories, dressers, and bureaus all received fitted covers or embroidered scarves. Needlework ran rife over slippers, suspenders, purses, and other articles of apparel. By the third quarter of the nineteenth century the fashion for home needlework had waned. The causes of this decline were complex: improvement in the quality of machine-made articles, the increasing ability of women to find scope for their energies outside the home, and changing styles in interior decoration that called for a lighter, less cluttered look. Of course, the production of hand needlework never ceased entirely, and, in fact, a number of efforts to keep fine needlework alive as an art form were launched in the latter part of the nineteenth century and early in the twentieth. Among these were the English School of Art Needlework at South Kensington, chiefly devoted to translating the medieval-inspired designs of William Morris and Edward Burne-Jones into needlework, and the Royal School of Needlework. In America the Needlework School of the Boston Museum of Fine Arts was

founded in 1879 and operated until World War I, and the Deerfield Society of Blue and White Needlework revived ancient forms and methods as a cottage industry between the end of the nineteenth century and 1926.

But not until recently did needlework enjoy the mass appeal that it had in the mid-nineteenth century. Again, new materials were part of the reason for this resurgent popularity—in particular, the introduction of Persian yarns with their wonderful color range and their adaptability to many kinds of needlework. Again, as the range and variety of mass-produced articles have become increasingly limited, many of us look for ways of expressing ourselves creatively, perhaps baking our own bread, making our own clothes, or stitching our own needlework. In doing so we often turn to the past for inspiration, perhaps through nostalgia but also for precedent.

Certainly the past with its antique objects is an almost endless source of inspiration for creative needlework. I used a number of different types of sources for the projects in this book. Of course, antique needlework was one of them. The tiger footstool, the crewel hangings, the bargello purse, and the picture based on a bed rug are all derived from authentic, dated, antique examples. But other kinds of antiques also have a rich vein of inspiration to offer. For the projects in this book I have also used fabric and textiles, a rug, wallpaper, porcelain, and tinware. If you look around you—in your home, in museums, in antique shops—you will undoubtedly find numerous other objects that could serve as inspiration for your own creative needlework. How you use antique-design sources depends to some extent on why you are making a particular piece of needlework. If it is to be part of the restored furnishings of an historic house or to go with authentic period furnishings in your own home, you may wish to follow an antique model quite closely. If, however, you are using antiques as source material just because you like them, you have a lot more flexibility. Don't hesitate, for instance, to change color schemes to match your own decor. The original William Morris wallpaper was printed in pinks and greens, but it is equally effective in the oranges and blue-greens that were used for the chair seat. You can adapt it to your own color scheme. Most antique needlework was made in the days before commercial dry cleaning was available, which is why, except for pictures, dark colors were usually chosen for the background. With Scotchgard and modern cleaning methods you don't need to be quite as practical and can choose light shades if they suit your taste.

Of course, needlework based on an antique of a particular era will go well with pieces from the same period. For each project I have given the exact or approximate date when the piece on which it was based was made. But don't feel confined to using needlework based on antiques only in a period setting: the designs based on the quilt and the coverlet, for example, would look as good in a contemporary room as with the early nineteenth-century furnishings for which they were first made.

Any home can stand only so many needlework pillows or pictures! I have tried to illustrate many other uses to which you can put your needlework, both in the way the designs in this book can be made up and in the suggestions for other uses of each design. Don't hesitate to adapt designs to your own needs.

Having needlework mounted and made up into a finished piece can be expensive, but you can learn to do a great deal of this work yourself. I have included step-by-step instructions for each project in this book, not just for the needlework but for turning it into upholstered pieces, curtains, articles of clothing, and well-made pillows.

Finding inspiration in the past for our own needlework today can be very satisfying for those of us who love both antiques and our craft. The quest for sources, in your own home or friends' homes, in books, or in museums, is stimulating in itself. Whether your aim is authenticity or adding the spice of variety to furnishings of any period, antiques can be an endless source of ideas for designs, textures, and colors.

2. MATERIALS, STITCHES, AND TECHNIQUES

In recent years people have become more and more dissatisfied with the practice of furnishing their homes and clothing their bodies with the impersonal products of a computerized machine age. More and more they want to surround themselves with the products of their own hands—not just for the products themselves, which are usually far better-looking and longer-lasting than storebought goods (if they can be bought at all) but also for the pure joy in the rhythm of stitching, for the feel of the materials they are working with, for the sight of the design taking shape with each movement of the needle, for the pleasure of something to do in their leisure hours, and for the pride of accomplishment when the work is framed, sewn up, or upholstered and admired by others.

Because so much time, energy, skill, care, and money are involved in the needlework projects that you choose to stitch, spending a few cents more at the beginning for the finest-quality supplies will help to ensure fine products at the finish. If you use inferior supplies for needlework, you may end up with the disaster of torn canvas or fabric threads, misshapen canvases or fabrics that won't block out square, or yarns that pill, fuzz, catch, wear thin quickly, or, worst of all, bleed.

MATERIALS
Needles

Needles for counted-thread embroidery (needlepoint on canvas and cross-stitch on even-weave cotton or linen) differ from those for free, or crewel, embroidery. In counted-thread embroidery the needle should not actually pierce the fabric or canvas but pass through the holes between the woven fabric or canvas threads. Therefore, blunt-tipped needles with large eyes, called tapestry needles, are used. They are available in sizes 13 (large) to 26 (very small). Needles for crewel embroidery have long, narrow eyes, which do not allow the thread to slip, and sharp tips to pierce the fabric. They are available in sizes 1 (large) through 10 (small). The size of the needle you choose to work with will depend largely on the weight of the thread you are using and the cloth that you stitch on. The needle must prepare the hole in the cloth for the thread to pass comfortably through but must not leave a hole too large, or your stitches will slip around and not stay where you place them.

Chenille needles have large eyes like tapestry needles and sharp tips like crewel needles. They are useful for heavier weights of wool in crewel embroidery and are sized on the same scale as tapestry needles.

Thimbles

Most traditional needlework books state that you cannot do fine embroidery without a thimble. Others do not mention a thimble at all, apparently assuming that it is as intrinsic to embroidery as a needle. Indeed, some people absolutely cannot pick up a needle without using a thimble—others literally cannot pick up a needle with a thimble! If you do use one, make sure that it fits properly, or it will be no help at all. My mother, who taught me how to sew and embroider and for years tried to keep a thimble on my finger, carries hers in her purse wherever she goes, even though she does not always carry a needle and thread. She feels that she can find a needle and thread anywhere if she needs them, but a good-fitting thimble is hard to find. There is no middle ground in speaking about thimbles. You either love them or hate them.

Frames and Hoops

Whether or not to use a hoop to keep needlework taut while it is being stitched is not quite as arbitrary as whether or not to use a thimble. A frame is totally unnecessary for needlepoint if the majority of the work is stitched in the basket-weave stitch, which distorts the canvas very little if at all. It was probably the widespread use of the basket-weave stitch (which freed needlepoint from the encumbrance of a frame and made it portable) that led to needlepoint's recent nationwide popularity. If, on the other hand, the majority of the work is done with the Continental stitch or other stitches that greatly distort the canvas, a frame is definitely needed, and even then there will be some distortion. Most canvases need to be blocked somewhat when they are completed. The use of a frame ensures that only one blocking will be needed to square the canvas up again instead of two or even three blockings. Even then a very distorted canvas that is not permanently mounted on a board or stretcher may crawl back out of shape.

Rugs of any size should be worked on a frame. The sheer weight and bulk of this kind of project make it impossible to work in the hand. The rug in the coverlet pattern shown in figure 3-33 was worked on a frame and needed absolutely no blocking when it was completed. Blocking a rug at home requires either a board larger than the rug itself or an attic floor that you don't mind making holes in, at least two people to pull and tug, and lots and lots of pushpins or tacks. It is far wiser to invest in a rug frame with the two roller bars and leg stretcher a little bit longer than the rug is wide so that the entire rug can be accommodated on the frame at the same time.

Frames or hoops are absolutely essential to most kinds of free embroidery. Keeping the fabric taut in the hoop or frame prevents it from puckering and keeps the stitches neat and even. Even embroidery stitches that don't need a frame to keep them even and neat will benefit from the use of a hoop, if only to keep the working area clear of all the other fabric. For this kind of work keep the material a little loose in the hoop so that you can sew with one motion instead of stabbing up and down with two motions.

Embroidery hoops come in sets of two circular or oval shapes. The fabric is placed over the inner hoop, then the outer hoop is pushed down over the fabric and the inner hoop so that the fabric stays taut between the two parts. This is accomplished by means of a screw or spring fitted on the outer part of the hoop. Choose a hoop made of wood or plastic with a screw on the outer ring to keep the fabric stretched really tightly without slipping.

Embroidery, needlepoint, and rug frames are larger than hoops. Once the work is secured on the frame, it is held until the entire piece is finished. In contrast, with a hoop the work can be moved to another section at any time. Frames are rectangular in shape with two rotating bars that roll up finished areas of work and unroll unstitched areas to make them accessible.

Unless your hoop or frame is mounted on some sort of stand, you will have to hold it with one hand and do all your stitching with two motions of the other hand. There are many kinds of hoops and frames that have extensions that either clamp to a table, sit on the floor or on a table, or slip underneath your body while you sit, thus freeing both hands for the two-handed above-and-below stabbing motion that makes embroidery with a frame go much faster. The sit-upon, or fanny, frame is the only portable type of frame or hoop with a stand.

A third type of frame, which is nicely suited to needlework intended to hang on the wall, is the artist's canvas-stretcher frame, sold in art-supply stores. It is inexpensive and comes in individual pieces, two for the length and two for the width, which you snap together to form a square or rectangle. To use a stretcher frame, mount the unworked fabric as though it were a finished piece being readied for framing. Instructions are given in the section on mounting and framing later in this chapter. Work the embroidery in the stretcher and buy ready-made framing strips to frame the work at home and save the considerable expense of sending your work out to a framing shop. Just be sure when you buy the stretcher frame to leave a large enough margin of unembroidered fabric to cover the wooden part of the frame so that you can stitch right up to it.

Other Supplies

It is essential to have among your needlework supplies a sharp pair of scissors with pointed tips, which should be used exclusively for cutting threads. A good way to make sure that they are always handy when you are working—and, incidentally, to let the rest of the family know that they are your special scissors and are not to be borrowed—is to tie the two ends of a long, heavy cord, braid, or length of rug yarn to the two finger holes. The scissors can then be hung around your neck for easy access while you are stitching. For cutting material or canvas use larger cutting shears, not embroidery scissors.

You will also need a yardstick or a tapemeasure (be sure to use the kind that will not stretch) and a small 6" ruler. Regular sewing thread and needles should be handy too.

To keep your working threads neat and easily accessible, not tangled up in your embroidery basket or bag, loosely knot the working lengths of cotton or wool over the inside ring of an unused embroidery hoop. Your threads can be arranged in color families so there will be no question as to whether to use the second or perhaps the third shade in each range. There are many yarn palettes on the market now, which hold the working threads in the same way as the inexpensive embroidery hoop. They are shaped like the traditional artist's palette but have holes around the outer edges through which the threads are knotted.

If you are working on a large piece in your hand

rather than in a frame, you may want to have some large safety pins or diaper pins to keep the worked sections neatly rolled up and out of the way. Rolling large pieces up in this way also makes it easier to get your hand around the work when it has to be turned.

Fabrics

The type of stitching that you intend to do and the purpose that you ultimately intend it to serve will largely determine the type of fabric you choose to work on. For upholstery and draperies linen or a linen-and-cotton blend is the best choice. These articles are usually quite large and therefore represent a sizable investment in time and expense. You want the fabric to be as durable as possible, and linen for countless centuries has been the fabric of choice for that very reason. It also has the advantage of holding each individual stitch securely in place without slipping or moving other stitches. Linen fabrics specially woven for crewel embroidery, in either plain, square basket weave, or diagonally ribbed twill weave, are sold in fine needlework shops. These are very expensive and for most of us within our budgets only for small individual pieces such as purses or chair seats or for upholstery that will receive a great deal of wear. For other large projects such as curtains or draperies it is worthwhile to investigate other fabrics. In stores with large drapery- and upholstery-fabric departments you may find suitable fabrics at a much lower cost—for instance, I found a natural-colored linen-and-cotton blend (60/40 ratio) with a slight slub that makes it look like a homespun fabric, 54" wide and on sale at less than $3 a yard. At antique auctions and shops, flea markets, rummage sales, and yard sales whole cartons of linen-homespun sheets and other old fabrics are sometimes sold at very low prices. Some of these may be suitable for embroidery if they are in good shape with no rips, holes, or stains. Keep your eyes open but be careful.

For counted-thread embroidery such as cross-stitch samplers the fabric you choose will depend on many factors. Your first consideration must be your design. After you have graphed the design, calculate how wide and how long the stitched area will be by counting the number of squares on the graph paper and multiplying by two (assuming that you plan to do each cross-stitch over two fabric threads). The figure thus obtained will tell you the minimum number of fabric threads needed in each dimension to accommodate the design area. Decide how large you want the sampler to be and try to find an even-weave linen fabric with countable threads to fit those dimensions. Look for fabrics with 18 to 32 threads per inch. Most good needlework shops have them. If your graphed area is about 200 cross-stitches square, you will need at least 400 fabric threads in each dimension to accommodate the design. A fabric with 18 threads to the inch will end up about 20" square, while a fabric with 32 threads per inch will be about 12" square using the same design chart. To find these measurements, divide the number of fabric threads needed by the number of fabric threads per inch. Just be sure that the fabric you choose has the same number of fabric threads in each direction, or your design will be elongated in the direction with the fewest threads per inch. Be sure to purchase enough fabric to allow at least 3" of unworked margin on each side. For a 15"-square sampler you should have at least 21" of fabric. Another consideration in buying your fabric is whether or not there will be any areas of free embroidery along with the cross-stitch. If so, your fabric should have a fairly high thread count.

For embroidery on clothing your prime consideration in choosing the fabric should be its suitability. Will it drape properly, or is it too stiff or limp? Will it wash well, or will it have to be sent out to the cleaner? You must ask if it is woven firmly enough to accept stitches easily and hold them in place. Some of the newer synthetic fibers are so strong and durable (a very desirable quality) that passing the needle and thread through them is quite difficult (a very undesirable quality). Look for blends of natural and synthetic fibers, such as polyester combined with cotton or wool.

Canvas

Needlepoint is simply embroidery on canvas. Many different stitches and yarns may be used. All needlepoint stitches are based on counting the threads of the canvas. Unlike free embroidery, or crewel, the entire surface of the canvas is covered with stitches, which, because of their dependence on the canvas, are uni-form in size, direction, and shape.

Two types of canvas are commonly used in needlepoint, mono and Penelope. Although at one time they were made of linen, they are now generally available only in cotton.

Mono canvas (figure 2-1) is the more commonly used type. It is loosely woven of single threads with large holes or spaces between the thread intersections or crossings. This makes it easy on the eyes when working. There is no doubt as to where to place each stitch, as there sometimes is with Penelope canvas. Besides plain mono canvas there is a relatively recent addition to the market called interlocking mono canvas. It is a lighter-weight canvas, more heavily starched or sized, and has the advantage of locking each horizontal and vertical thread crossing in place.

Penelope canvas (figure 2-2) is woven with evenly spaced horizontal, or weft, threads, which are crossed by closely spaced vertical, or warp, threads. In some Penelope canvases, especially in large-gauge or rug canvases, the warp and weft spacings are reversed.

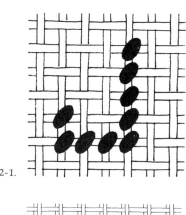

2-1.

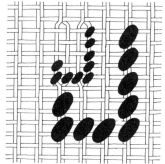

2-2.

These double threads can be stitched as is, over the four-thread intersection, or pricked apart to accommodate tiny stitches over each two-thread intersection. The tiny stitches are called petit point; the larger stitches, gros point. Most rugs should be made with Penelope canvas, because the added strength of the double threads is needed for the hard wear a rug usually receives.

Whichever canvas you choose, it should be of superior quality. The threads should be highly polished to allow the yarn to slide between them easily. The canvas should also be sized or starched to keep the stitching even. It should not have any knots, although even in some of the best canvas you may encounter a knot here and there. If so, try to plan your needlework so that the knots fall in the unworked margin. If that is impossible, put a spot of white glue on the knot to keep it from pulling out when the finished piece is blocked and mounted. Sometimes it is possible to put the knot on the underside of the project so that no bump will appear on the surface.

Both types of canvas come in different mesh sizes, or gauges. A 10-mesh canvas has 10 threads per inch, 100 per square inch. Since tent stitch, the most popular needlepoint stitch, is worked over single-thread intersections (on mono canvas), there will be 10 tent stitches per inch, 100 per square inch. The most popular mono-canvas sizes are 10, 12, 14, 16 (mostly for Bargello), and 18 (for petit point).

The mesh of the canvas will determine the finished size of the project if it is worked from a graph-paper chart. Each symbol on a chart usually refers to a single tent stitch on any mesh canvas. To find out how large any chart will work up on the canvas size you choose, divide the number of meshes per inch into the number of squares on the chart in each direction. For instance, if you have chosen a chart that is 200 squares wide × 300 squares high, your finished needlepoint would be approximately 20″ × 30″ on 10-mesh canvas, 16½″ × 25″ on 12-mesh canvas, 14″ × 21½″ on 14-mesh canvas, 12½″ × 18½″ on 16-mesh canvas, and 11″ × 16½″ on 18-mesh canvas. Adjustments have to be made for stitches that take more than one canvas thread. If you wish to work the same chart in cross-stitch over two threads on mono canvas, multiply the number of squares in the chart in

each direction by two to get the finished size. For instance, the same chart of 200 × 300 squares would work up to 40″ × 60″ on 10-mesh mono canvas, 22″ × 33″ on 18-mesh canvas.

Yarn

The yarn used for needlepoint must be strong enough to take the repeated journeys through the canvas without fraying and getting thin as the work progresses. It must be able to be moistened and pulled back into its original shape during the blocking process, and it should be able to take years of wear without getting fuzzy, wearing through to the canvas, fading, or becoming food for moths. The soft, springy knitting yarns made of short wool fibers cannot fulfill all of those requirements and will not cover the canvas evenly.

Paternayan Paterna Persian wool yarn, the most popular and most widely available needlepoint yarn in the country, fulfills all these requirements. It is made of long fibers, and, although it is a bit hairy, it is also soft, lustrous, and long-wearing. In 1929 the Paternayan brothers began a 5-year search for a wool yarn to repair antique Persian rugs and weave new ones. They finally blended just the right yarns for this purpose and started dyeing them in their own dye house, and today there are almost 350 colors, many in families of up to seven shades, for even and lifelike modeling and shading. At first many of the finest shops guarded the name and source of the yarn, but little by little the needlepointers of the world found that the qualities that made this fine yarn perfect for Persian rugs also made it perfect for their own purposes, and the company took away the veil of secrecy and began distributing it nationally. Recently ·Brunswick, Bucilla, Paragon, and Bon Pasteur have put their own brands of Persian wool on the market. There is even an acrylic Persian-type yarn, just what the doctor ordered for needleworkers who are allergic to wool.

Because Persian yarn is three-ply (three strands of thread twisted loosely together), it can be used as is in the needle or stripped down to two-ply or even one-ply for fine stitching. The number of strands you use in your needle will depend on the stitch you decide to use and the mesh of canvas you stitch on. One word of caution: when you work with two plies in the needle, the two strands will be twisted, while the ply left over from splitting the full strand will be untwisted when used in the needle with another leftover ply. Therefore two-thirds of the canvas will be worked with twisted yarn, while one-third will be worked with untwisted yarn. To maintain a uniform surface, separate or untwist the two plies left after stripping away the third ply.

The mesh size of the canvas you choose and the stitch you use determine how many plies to use in the needle. Your main objective is to cover the canvas completely with relaxed stitches. The table shown below is helpful but should not be taken as an absolute rule. If you find that you are having trouble covering the canvas, you may be stitching very tightly and may need one more ply to do an adequate job, although it would be better to loosen up your stitching. For other stitches experiment in a corner to see just how many plies you need.

Mesh Canvas	Persian-yarn Plies	Needle Size
18 mono	1-ply for tent stitch	22
	2-ply for Bargello	
16 mono	2-ply for Bargello	20
14 mono	2-ply for tent stitch	19
	3-ply for Bargello	
12 mono	2-ply for tent stitch	18
	3-ply for Bargello	
10 mono	3-ply for tent stitch	18
	4-5-ply for Bargello	
5 Penelope	6-ply for cross-stitch	13
	or 1 strand of rug	
	yarn for tent stitch	

Once you have decided on the mesh of canvas for the size of your project, you have to decide how much yarn to buy. It is better to buy more than enough yarn to start with than to run out and have to go back for more. Leftover yarns can be used for sampler projects.

The chart shown in figure 2-3 estimates the minimum amount of yarn you will need for any project. Most stores sell Persian yarn by the ounce, sometimes by the strand if only one or two strands of a particular color are needed. One full strand of Paterna Persian yarn (a skein cut through once) is not quite 2 yards. Two yards will cover approximately 1½ square inches on any size of canvas. At about 20 strands per ounce there are around 320 strands per pound. One pound will cover 480 square inches. With these figures as a basis the graph will prove useful in computing the amount of yarn necessary to complete a canvas. To find out how many square inches your project is, multiply the length by the width.

After you have figured out the total amount of yarn you need, divide that amount into design colors and background color. Unfortunately there is no formula for this: you must estimate, so overestimate and you won't come up short. And just think of all the Christmas ornaments, eyeglass cases, buttons, pockets, and other small articles you can make with your leftovers.

Before Persian yarn became available only 25 years ago, the most widely used yarn for needlepoint was four-ply tapestry yarn. It was sold mainly for filling in the backgrounds of canvases in which the design was prestitched, a rather dishonest (not to mention boring) way of getting a piece of needlepoint into the home. But enough said about that! Tapestry yarn looks like a tightly twisted knitting yarn and doesn't have the luster of Persian yarn. It is still available and works well on 10- or 12-mesh canvas. It can be split in half into two two-ply strands for finer work.

Silk and other shiny threads should be used with discretion in canvaswork. They are most useful for adding highlights and small details or for a change in texture. Silk threads are difficult to begin and finish

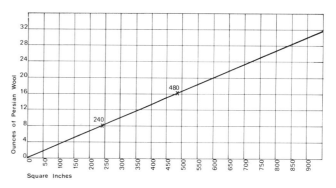

2-3.

off in the usual way—by running the ends into the back of the work—unless they are run into a nearby wool yarn. Silk is slippery and tends to bump in the needle. It also tangles easily, so great care must be taken to keep the work neat. For these reasons each needleful should be a relatively small length—say, 8″ or 10″. Silk for embroidery is not available in many shops. Some other shiny threads that can be used in its place are silk buttonhole twist (available at most fabric stores in 10-yard spools), pearl cotton, and stranded embroidery cotton, or cotton floss. None of these threads is as durable as wool and should not be used if it will receive hard wear. If you want to use one of them anyway, stitch it on top of existing wool stitches. If it does disintegrate, the bare canvas will not show through, although, since the shiny thread is raised above the surface, it will receive hard wear before the lower and more durable wool thread. There is no real solution except to restitch it if it goes.

Like the Persian wool used for needlepoint, crewel wool is made of long fibers for durability. The fibers are twisted into two-ply strands, slightly lighter than a single ply of Persian wool, and may be used for both crewel and needlepoint on both fine- and coarse-mesh canvases. A single strand of Persian wool may also be used for crewel embroidery with the same fine results.

For years embroidery on clothing meant using six-strand cotton embroidery thread. It was divisible, which meant that you could make it thicker or thinner to suit a particular purpose; it came in hundreds of colors and was available everywhere, even the local five-and-ten; and most important, it was washable. It is still available, but now there is D.M.C. pearl cotton, which is a twisted thread with a beautiful high gloss. It comes in weights ranging from 1 (the thickest) to 8 (the finest) and is incredibly easy to work with. It hardly ever tangles, and, since it is a single strand, it cannot bump in the needle. It comes in almost as many colors as six-strand floss, and although it is not as readily available as the floss, some local dime stores have a limited color range. Most people, once introduced to pearl cotton, swear never to return to the floss. It is well worth the trouble you may have in finding it. Another advantage of pearl cotton is that, besides small skeins, it is also available in 53- to 95-yard balls.

STITCHES

Although many of the designs in this book may seem intricate, the needlework itself is relatively uncomplicated, and in most cases even the novice or intermediate will be able to stitch beautiful pieces. A short refresher course in stitchery is provided for those who are not quite sure of their skills. It may also strengthen the skills of the more advanced or remind them of stitches that they haven't worked in a while.

Stitches can be broadly grouped into those used for counted-thread embroidery and those used for free embroidery. In counted-thread embroidery the background fabric or canvas is used to count the stitches precisely, to place them in the proper order, and to make sure that they are uniform in size. In free embroidery the fabric is usually tightly woven and forms a background only: the size, number, and direction of the stitches is dictated by the motif. Since the stitches for free embroidery can sometimes be used for counted-thread work, I have arranged all the stitches in alphabetical order; the following table indicates how they are usually used.

Counted-thread Stitches	Free-embroidery Stitches
Algerian eye	backstitch
binding stitch	bullion knot
brick stitch	buttonhole or blanket stitch
cross-stitch	chain stitch
flame stitch or Bargello	whipped chain stitch
mosaic stitch	cloud filling
flat stitch	couched filling
Scotch stitch	Cretan stitch
tent stitch	feather stitch
Continental stitch	French knot
basket-weave stitch	herringbone stitch
	laced spiderweb
	lazy daisy
	long-and-short stitch
	Pekinese stitch
	raised chain band
	satin stitch
	stem or outline stitch
	Van Dyck stitch

I have described only the stitches used for the projects in this book. You may want to personalize the projects by choosing other stitches. Many books are devoted entirely to stitches and can be used for inspiration. Left-handed needleworkers will find the directions easier to follow if they trace the illustrations onto tracing paper and read the diagrams from the reverse side of the tracings.

Algerian Eye

The Algerian-eye stitch (figure 2-4) can be used as a filling or as a border stitch. It is actually a series of eight stitches taken around a square of four canvas threads, each stitch going into the same center hole. Work clockwise around the square. When each unit is completed, run your working thread through the stitches on the back to secure it before moving on to the next unit.

In working Algerian eye on counted-thread fabric, the working threads may be pulled tightly to form holes at the center points. Be sure that you do not cover the hole as you move from stitch to stitch.

Backstitch

The backstitch (figure 2-5) is one of the simplest and most useful embroidery stitches. It is the basis for many other stitches and can be whipped, threaded singly or doubly, or laced to vary the effect. All the stitches must be the same size for the best effect.

Working from right to left, bring the needle and thread out at A, which should not be at the edge of the motif but a short distance away. Insert the needle at B, which should be at the edge a short distance to the right, take a longer stitch to the left, and come out at C. Reinsert the needle at A. The distance from A to B should equal the distance from A to C. Notice also that the stitch on the back is twice as long as the stitch on the front. For a clear, crisp line, especially on a curve, keep the stitches quite small.

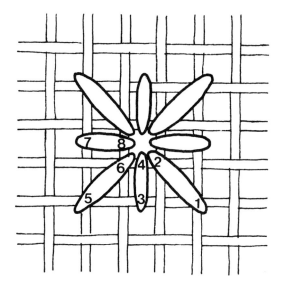

2-4.

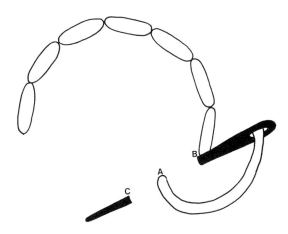

2-5.

Binding Stitch

Binding stitch (figures 2-6, 2-7, and 2-8) is a useful stitch that all needlepointers should include in their repertoire. It is used to finish off the edges of any piece of needlepoint without machine sewing or adding a cloth binding and to join two separate pieces of needlepoint together with an attractive and durable braided edge.

To finish off a single piece of needlepoint, work the binding stitch over the selvedge if the interior has been worked right up to it. If there is excess canvas, cut off the selvedge and fold back the excess canvas so that two or more unworked threads remain on top. The number of unworked threads left on top will determine how wide the bound edge will be.

To join two separate pieces of needlepoint, fold back the unworked canvas on each piece so that only one canvas thread is on top. Place the two pieces with the wrong sides facing each other and work the binding stitch through both pieces. Make sure there are exactly the same number of canvas threads on each piece to be joined.

Holding the needlepoint with the right side facing you and working from left to right, whip over the edge three times using four successive holes, each time bringing the needle from the back to the front. Go back and bring the needle from back to front through hole A. Move forward and bring the needle out at hole E. Move back to hole B, then forward to hole F. Continue in this manner along the entire edge, moving forward into empty holes, backwards into previously worked holes.

The progression from holes A to E, B to F, and C to G creates a very heavy edge suitable for binding the edges of rugs. For less heavy edges use the progression from hole A to D, B to E, and C to F or even from A to C, B to D, and C to E. Although the illustrations show the braided crossings on the front for the sake of clarity, in actuality the crossings are on the edge.

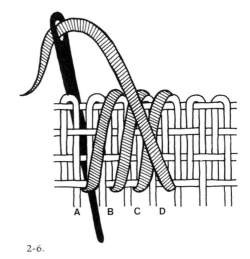

2-6.

2-7.

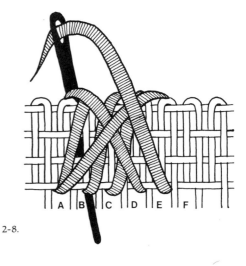

2-8.

Brick Stitch

Brick stitch (figure 2-9) is a straight, upright stitch taken over two canvas threads or four fabric threads. The first row is worked from right to left, skipping a space between the stitches. The space is half filled by the second row of stitches, which is worked from left to right. The leftover half space at the top of the first row is filled in with small stitches as the first row progresses or when the work is finished. Continue working the rows from right to left, then left to right. Notice that the needle is always brought out of an empty hole and inserted into a shared hole. Brick stitch is an excellent background stitch, and it makes a smooth filling on counted-thread fabric.

Bullion Knot

Bullion knot (figure 2-10) is a complicated stitch employed mainly for small petals and leaves, but it can also be used to form entire small flowers by looping a few stitches around each other. For the latter procedure, called the Puerto Rico rose stitch, the stitch should be longer than the space allotted to it so that the knot will arch up slightly from the fabric.

Bring the needle and thread out at A. Insert the needle at B and bring it halfway out at A again, leaving a loop of thread on the surface between A and B. Holding the needle under the material with the right hand, twist the long section of thread remaining above the material around the needle with the left hand; the number of loops to make depends on the space between A and B and whether the finished stitch is to lie flat or arch up. Keeping your left hand on the loops to regulate the tension, coax the needle through the loops with the right hand. As you pull the needle and thread through the loops, the coil will fall over to fill the space between A and B. Reinsert the needle at B to finish.

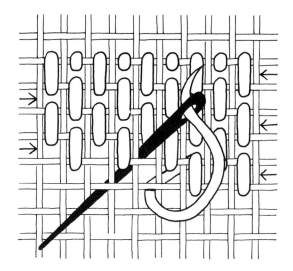

2-9.

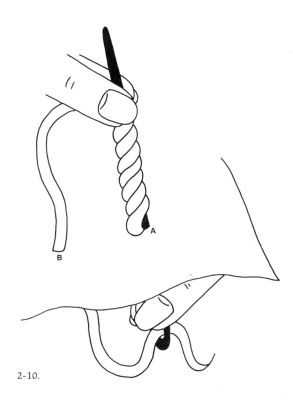

2-10.

21

Buttonhole or Blanket Stitch

Buttonhole stitch (figure 2-11) is the simplest of the family of looped stitches, a row of straight stitches with a looped lower edge. It is easily worked freehand without a frame or hoop. Working from left to right, bring the thread out at A. Insert the needle at B and bring the thread out at C, directly below B, keeping a loop of thread under the needle from A to B. Pull through, reinsert the needle at D, and pull through at E, holding a loop of thread from C to D under the needle.

When the stitches are spaced farther apart, as in figure 2-11, they are called blanket stitches; when the stitches are worked close together, buttonhole stitches. To fill in shapes, stitches of varying lengths can be placed in groups, with one row of stitches overlapping the row above it (figure 2-12). To make a buttonhole- or blanket-stitch filling, work from right to left, then from left to right, piercing the material with each stitch.

Buttonhole stitch can also be used for shading (figure 2-13). Work each row through the loops of the preceding row. Each row or couple of rows can be worked in another color for a softly shaded filling.

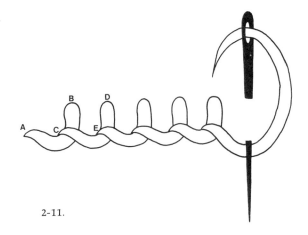

2-11.

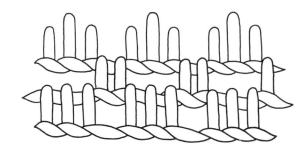

2-12.

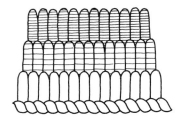

2-13.

Chain and Whipped-chain Stitches

Chain stitch (figure 2-14) is the simplest in a series of increasingly complex chained stitches. It may be used as a line stitch or as a solid filling for shapes with a smooth surface. It is simply a series of loops, each subsequent loop anchoring the preceding one in the line. The great beauty of chain stitch lies in its regularity, so keep your stitches flat and the same length. Do not pull too tightly or your material will pucker.

Come out at A, which should be at the top of the line. On curved lines turn your fabric gradually so that you are always working from top to bottom. Hold a loop of thread down with the left thumb and reinsert the needle at A. Come out at B, a short distance away from and directly below A, and draw the thread through, holding the loop down under the needle. Repeat the above procedure at B and so on. The back of the work should show a series of little backstitches.

Chain stitch, like many other stitches, may be whipped with the same or a contrasting color of thread (figure 2-15). Use a blunt-tipped tapestry needle. Come out at the top and pass the needle from right to left under each entire chain stitch, taking care not to pierce the fabric. Each side of the stitch can also be whipped separately.

The small stitch at the bottom of figure 2-15 ties down not only the last stitch but the entire line. If it were not there, the line could be unraveled like a line of crochet chain. Be sure that every line of chain stitch is similarly tied down at the end.

Cloud Filling

Cloud filling (figure 2-16) is a pretty but simple composite stitch for filling shapes. First work a series of relaxed small, upright, straight stitches, alternately spaced in rows over the area to be filled. Change to a blunt-tipped tapestry needle and with the same or a contrasting color of thread lace through the small stitches in a zigzag manner from row to row. The lacing thread pierces the fabric only at the beginning and end of each row.

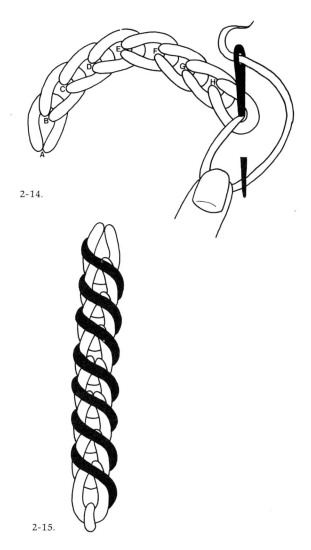

2-14.

2-15.

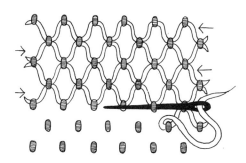

2-16.

23

Couched Filling Stitch

Couched filling stitch (figure 2-17) can cover large areas of any shape with a light, open filling that is neater than other filling stitches. A hoop or frame is essential. The space to be filled is first covered by a grid of long, regularly spaced stitches that pass from one side of the shape to the other. These long stitches may be either straight or on the diagonal. They are then couched, or tied down to the fabric, at each intersection with either tent stitch or cross-stitch. The spaces of fabric that show between the long couched threads may be left bare or filled with French knots, upright cross-stitches, or any other small, isolated stitches. Figure 2-17 shows all these variations.

Many variations are also possible in the choice of color, weight of thread, and placement of the long threads. These may be doubled—two threads side by side with a small space between—they may be alternately heavy and light in weight; or a second set of long threads may be laid diagonally across after the first set has been tied down.

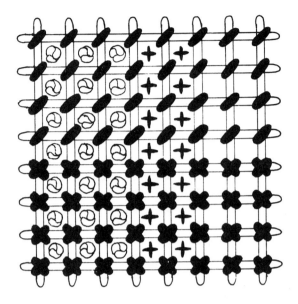

2-17.

Cretan Stitch

Cretan stitch (figure 2-18) is used to fill shapes and to stitch broad lines. The illustration shows a leaf-shaped filling; depending on the slant of the stitches and the distance between them, many varied effects may be obtained.

Bring the needle and thread out at the top of the shape or line at A (for a broad line A would be on the left). Insert the needle outside on the right at B and bring it out a little to the left at C, keeping the thread under the needle. Insert the needle at D and take a small stitch to the right, coming out at E and again keeping the thread under the needle. Continue crisscrossing in this manner.

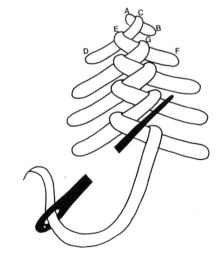

2-18.

24

Cross-stitch

Cross-stitch (figures 2-19 and 2-20) is one of the oldest stitches as well as one of the easiest. In many embroidery styles, especially Victorian canvaswork and samplers, it is the only stitch used.

The stitch can be done in two ways. In the first method the entire stitch is made at one time before moving on to the next stitch (figure 2-19). The thread emerges at A. The needle is inserted diagonally to the left over two canvas-thread intersections at B, then brought out straight down two canvas threads below at C. The thread then crosses the first half of the stitch and is inserted diagonally upward to the right over two canvas-thread intersections at D. Bring the needle out again at C (E) for the start of the next stitch.

In the second method the stitch is completed in two separate trips across the canvas, the first half of the stitch on the first trip, the second on the return journey (figure 2-20).

Working each stitch separately before moving on to the next provides a firmer backing, since there is both a straight stitch and a slanting stitch on the back. Working the stitch in two trips leaves only straight stitches, which do not completely cover the canvas, on the back.

Be sure that all cross-stitches are crossed in the same direction: traditionally the top half of the stitch slants from bottom left to top right, as in the natural slant of handwriting. All forms of tent stitch also slant in the same direction and may be combined easily with cross-stitch.

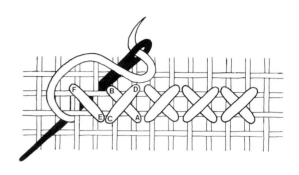

2-19.

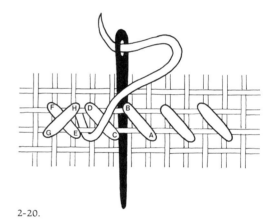

2-20.

Feather Stitch

Feather stitch (figure 2-21) is actually a large family of stitches, variations of which are suitable for continuous lines or for open fillings of leaves and such. The illustration shows the thorn, or briar, stitch worked over four lines. Working from the top down, bring the thread out at A on the left. Reinsert the needle to the right at B, bringing the thread out at C and holding the loop of thread from A to B under the needle. Insert the needle at D and bring the thread out at E, again holding the loop of thread from C to D under the needle. Continue in this manner.

Feather stitch can also be worked on a basis of two lines, three lines, or even five lines, with the stitches either far apart or touching, slanting or straight (figure 2-22).

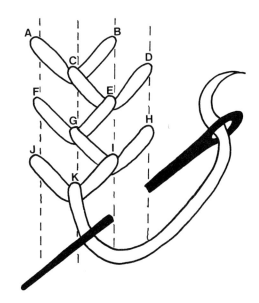

2-21.

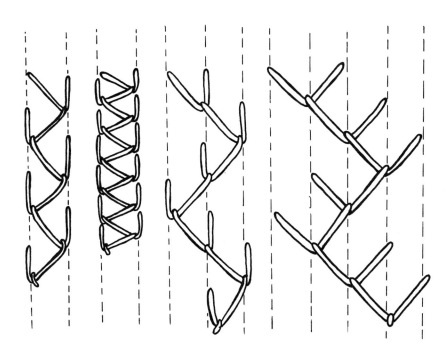

2-22.

26

Flame Stitch or Bargello

The type of canvas needlework variously known as Bargello, flame stitch, Florentine stitch, or Hungarian point is quick and easy to do, one reason for its continuing popularity. The other reason is its tremendous visual impact, which is greatest when it is worked in color families with several shades to each family.

Bargello is characteristically worked in vertical stitches over a preselected number of canvas threads in alternating diagonal rows (figure 2-23). The carnation pattern shown here is a four-two pattern: that is, each stitch covers four horizontal canvas threads and starts two threads higher or lower than the previous stitch. Many other combinations are possible. Notice that in moving upward from stitch to stitch the thread on the back of the canvas will be short, while it will be long when the stitches move downward. Work the rows alternately from right to left, then left to right.

In starting any Bargello piece, the most important step is to place the first row of stitches properly. When this row is properly counted and stitched, all of the following rows will fall neatly into place without further troublesome counting.

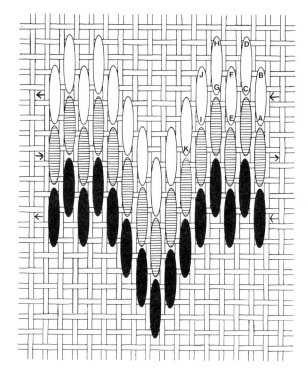

2-23.

French Knot

The French knot (figure 2-24) can be scattered over a surface as a powdered filling, packed closely together as a solid filling, or strung in a series to form a line. To stitch a line of knots, work from right to left. Using a hoop to hold the material tight will make the work easier.

Bring the needle and thread out at A, hold the thread down with the left thumb, and rotate the needle under the thread once or twice but no more. Three turns around the needle will produce a floppy knot that tends to fall over. To make a larger knot, use heavier thread. Continuing to hold the thread so that it remains twisted fairly tightly around the needle, reinsert the needle at B, directly beside the point at which it first emerged. Pull the needle and thread through the twists to the back of the material, leaving a knot on the surface.

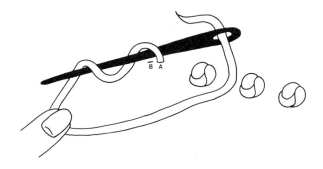

2-24.

Herringbone Stitch

Herringbone stitch (figure 2-25) is really a continuous line of interlaced cross-stitches with the crossings off-center. For a neat appearance all the diagonals should be parallel, and all the stitches regular in length, although they can be spaced close together or farther apart.

Work from left to right along an imaginary double line. Bring the thread out at A on the lower line. Reinsert the needle at B, a bit to the right on the upper line, and bring the thread out to the left at C. Insert the needle at D on the lower line, take another backstitch to the left, and bring the thread out at E. Repeat the preceding steps for a continuous line.

A variation of herringbone stitch, called closed herringbone or double backstitch, is made by bringing the thread out in the same place in which the needle was inserted in the previous stitch. Further variations can be made by lacing, threading, and tying the crossings.

2-25.

Laced Spiderweb

Laced spiderweb (figure 2-26) is an isolated stitch often used in crewel embroidery to depict berries and the centers of flowers.

Lay a circular foundation of four long stitches that cross in the center. With a blunt-tipped tapestry needle work a series of backstitches over the wheel spokes just formed. Do not pierce the fabric in lacing the web. Working counterclockwise, go over one spoke from left to right, then slide the needle under it and the next spoke to the left. Come up and over to the right, then under the second spoke and the next to its left. Continue in this manner, spiraling around the circle until the spokes are entirely filled.

For a raised effect the spokes of the wheel are worked loosely. They can be held up by looping a temporary thread under the center crossing while the backstitch lacing under the spokes is made. When the lacing is finished and the temporary thread is taken away, the finished web will stand domelike above the fabric.

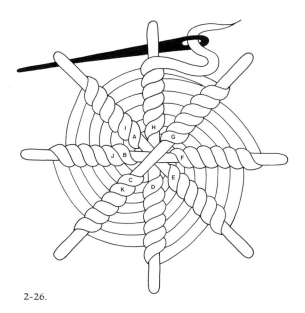

2-26.

Lazy-daisy Stitch

Lazy-daisy (figure 2-27) is a single detached chain stitch, held down with a small straight stitch that crosses over the middle of the loop. Lazy-daisy stitches may be scattered for a filling or worked around a circle to form a flower. Very small stitches can be used instead of French knots.

Long-and-short Stitch

Long-and-short stitch (figure 2-28) is one of the most frequently encountered stitches in crewel embroidery. It is a solid filling stitch that looks best and is most useful if it is worked in a graduated family of colors, from dark to light, for a softly shaded effect. In theory it is worked by starting from the outside of the shape to be filled and stitching down from the edge into the shape in a series of regularly placed long-and-short stitches. The short stitches should be about three-fourths the length of the long stitches. The next row fills in this line, working from the bottom up into the previously worked stitches. All the stitches in the second and following lines are not long and short but the same length as that of the longest stitches in the first row. Notice that the last row must be completed with small compensating stitches. All rows are stitched in alternating directions: left to right, then right to left.

In practice straight rows of stitches are rarely encountered. Since the stitch is usually used to make irregular shapes of leaves and petals, it is worked in a radiating fanlike fashion from the center or edge (figure 2-29). As more rows are filled in, the space to be filled becomes smaller and some stitches have to be missed, but it is especially important at this point to keep the stitches regular, making sure that the long-and-short sequence is continued for harmonious color shading. Once you decide how your stitches will run, it helps to lightly mark the lines on the material with pencil.

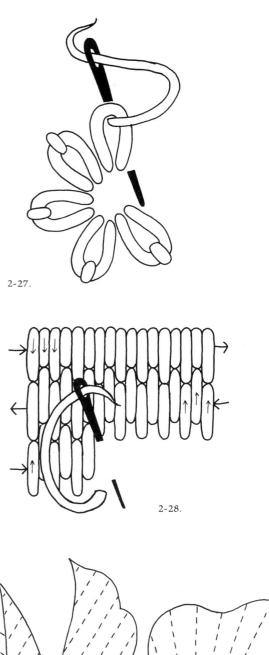

2-27.

2-28.

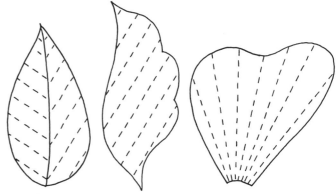

2-29.

Mosaic Stitch

Mosaic stitch is a lovely, fast-moving background stitch, which can be worked diagonally (figure 2-30), horizontally (figure 2-31), or vertically (figure 2-32). It is made by covering one canvas-thread intersection with two small tent stitches (figure 2-39) on either side of a large tent stitch, which covers two canvas-thread intersections. Together they form a neat square, covering two canvas threads in each direction. For a firm backing that does not distort the canvas, work the stitch in diagonal lines as with the basket-weave stitch (figure 2-44).

If you enlarge the mosaic stitch by adding longer, slanting stitches in the center to make a larger square, a variation known as flat stitch (figure 2-34) is formed. It can be worked over a square of three or four canvas threads. As a background stitch it is even faster to do than the mosaic stitch, but it is not as snagproof. Work it the same way as mosaic stitch: horizontally, vertically, or (preferably) diagonally.

By outlining squares of flat stitch with a network of Continental-stitch (figures 2-40 and 2-41) lines, Scotch stitch, another variation (figure 2-34) is formed. The Continental-stitch lines should be worked in steps starting at the top right and working to the bottom left, and the flat stitches should be filled in diagonally. Scotch stitch got its name because of its similarity to plaid designs, but it can also look like quilting. It was used on the Blazing Star quilt pattern for the background.

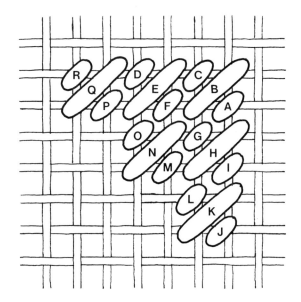

2-30.

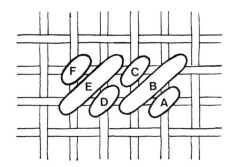

2-31.

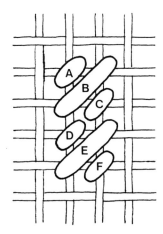

2-32.

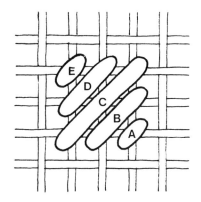

2-33.

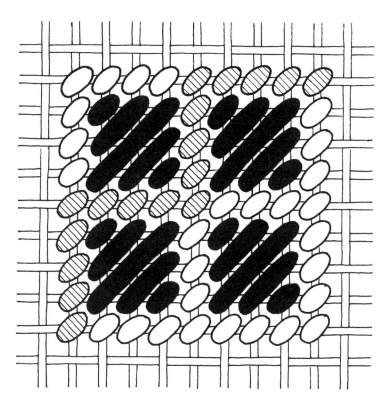

2-34.

Pekinese Stitch

Pekinese stitch (figure 2-35) is a composite stitch worked on a foundation of backstitches. It is highly effective for a single line, where it is braidlike in appearance, but was also used by the Chinese for entire pieces of embroidery. It is sometimes referred to in legend as the forbidden stitch: the story is that so many children went blind working intricately patterned and minutely stitched pieces of embroidery solely in Pekinese stitch that its use was subsequently forbidden.

First work a foundation of backstitches, which should not be pulled too tightly. Change to a blunt-tipped tapestry needle and, with the same or a contrasting color of thread, loop through each successive backstitch. For a tidy appearance, keep the loops fairly tight, especially in the lower portion of the piece.

2-35.

Raised Chain Band

Raised chain band (figure 2-36) is a composite stitch, actually an elaboration of the simple chain stitch. Although it may be worked in two colors like other composite stitches, its greatest value lies in the textural variation that it affords your embroidery.

First make a foundation of evenly spaced horizontal, straight stitches. The distance between and the length of the foundation threads depend on the thickness of the threads that you use and the desired effect. In any case do not place the stitches so far apart that the raised braid is lost. The foundation threads can be narrow enough not to show under the chains or wide enough to accommodate three separate rows of chains.

Change to a blunt-tipped tapestry needle and use the same or a contrasting color of thread. Bring the thread out at the top and do not pierce the fabric again until the end of the line. Slide the needle under the first foundation-thread bar from bottom to top, keeping it to the left. Slide the needle under the same bar, this time from top to bottom on the right side, keeping the loop just formed under the needle. Pull through and straight down. Continue in the same way on each foundation thread and secure the thread on the back.

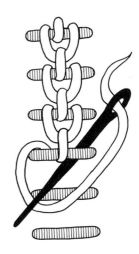

2-36.

Satin Stitch

Satin stitch (figure 2-37), a series of straight stitches laid close together side by side to fill a shape, looks easy but is in reality one of the most difficult stitches to do perfectly. The longer the stitch gets, the more prone it is to an untidy appearance. In many large single shapes such as leaves satin stitches are worked from the outside to a dividing line down the center, with the threads on each side of the centerline (either imaginary or stitched) changing direction. This change of direction adds a bit of dimension and a slight amount of shading to the smooth, lustrous look typical of satin stitch. Work the stitches diagonally, not straight, across the shape. A hoop or frame is essential.

Bring the needle out at the bottom of the shape and reinsert at the top. Bring the needle out again at the bottom as close as possible to the place at which it first emerged, retaining a sharp outline and keeping the threads lying neatly next to each other so that none of the material peeks through.

The shape to be filled may first be outlined with a simple line stitch such as chain, stem, or backstitch. Working the satin stitches over this edging helps to keep the outline sharp and tends to raise the satin stitches for a slightly padded effect.

Stem or Outline Stitch

Stem or outline stitch (figure 2-38) is one of the most useful of all embroidery stitches. It is usually used for lines such as stems and tendrils but can also be used for filling in shapes. In working the stitch the thread should always be held on the same side of the needle, or the spiral of the line will break and reverse direction. When the thread is held below the needle, the stitch is called a stem stitch; when held above the needle, outline stitch.

Work from left to right. Bring the needle and thread out at A and reinsert a short distance to the right at B. Bring the needle and thread out again halfway between A and B at C. Reinsert at D for the next stitch. A line of backstitch is formed on the back, and a tight spiral line on the front. For a broader or thicker line A and C should be slightly above the line, B and D slightly below the line. If the space between A and C and B and D gradually becomes wider, the stitch may imperceptibly blend into satin stitch.

In working the stitch around a curved line try to plan ahead so that the thread will be held on the outside of the curve in order to keep the line smooth. It also helps to make the stitches in the curve smaller than normal.

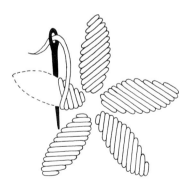

2-37.

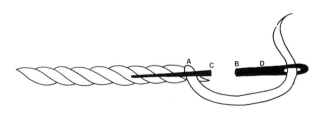

2-38.

Tent Stitch

Tent stitch (figure 2-39) in its various forms is the most widely used needlepoint stitch. On the surface it resembles half of a cross-stitch, and, although successive tent stitches may be made in a number of different ways, their appearance will change only on the back of the work.

The stitch is made by bringing the needle out (A), then reinserting it diagonally upward to the right over one canvas-thread intersection (B). All slanted stitches are variations of tent stitch and are always worked individually from bottom left to top right.

Half-cross-stitch, a tent-stitch variation, is exactly that, done on needlepoint canvas: It can only be worked on Penelope canvas, does not have a firm, well-padded back, and, like all diagonal stitches, distorts the canvas, so it is rarely used in most kinds of modern needlepoint.

Continental stitch is tent stitch worked in long rows, either horizontally (figure 2-40) or vertically (figure 2-41). The stitches on the back of the canvas are longer and more slanting than those on the front, and they provide a good padding for longer wear. The stitch does pull the canvas badly out of shape and so is used mainly for outlining areas to be filled in with basket-weave stitch or for long single lines of stitches. Because so much of the Victorian tiger design for the footstool shown in figure 3-54 had to be done in Continental stitch, it was worked in a frame and did not need much blocking.

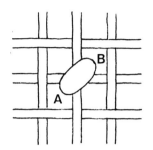

2-39.

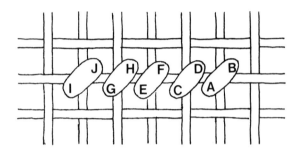

2-40.

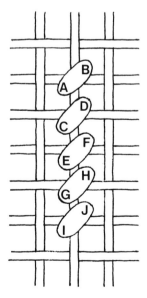

2-41.

Continental stitch starts on the right and moves towards the left; the canvas is turned around completely to start the next row. If you need another row, the section should probably be worked in basketweave, the next stitch described. To work Continental stitch vertically, start at the top and stitch toward the bottom, again turning the canvas for the next row. In working successive rows the needle always emerges at the bottom in a shared hole and is reinserted diagonally upward to the right into an empty hole. To work around a square (figure 2-42), start at the top right and work vertically down, then horizontally across to the left. Turn the canvas around completely and repeat the procedure.

In terms of design the only drawback of tent stitch is that two identical motifs on two sides of a centerline do not appear perfectly symmetrical because of the direction that each stitch takes. Because each stitch slants up and to the right, diagonal lines moving to the right appear continuous, while lines moving diagonally to the left appear to be broken by background-color stitches. Traditionally this problem has been overlooked in needlepoint, but if it disturbs you—and particularly in lettering—you can partially remedy it by stitching the lines that move up to the left in cross-stitch over a single-thread crossing, making sure that the top of the cross slants in the same direction as the regular tent stitches (figure 2-43). You will have to adjust your thread to prevent lumpy cross-stitches. If your tent stitches are worked with two yarn threads, use a single yarn thread for the cross-stitches. This method must be worked on interlocking mono or Penelope canvas, which does not allow the back of the first half-cross-stitch to slip under the thread crossing and get lost.

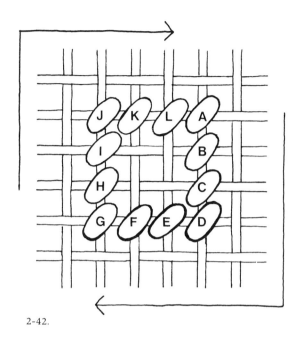

2-42.

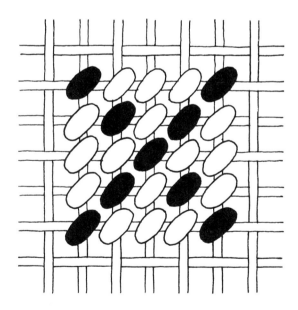

2-43.

Basket-weave stitch (figure 2-44) looks exactly the same as Continental stitch on the surface of the work. Each individual stitch is made in the same way as Continental stitch, but the method of traveling from one stitch to the next is quite different. A mesh of vertical and horizontal threads is formed on the back, like the weave of the canvas itself, creating the pattern which gives the stitch its name. This backing is firm and long-wearing. The stitch does not pull the canvas badly out of shape and should be used rather than Continental stitch wherever possible. It is also more fun to watch shapes fill up with color than simply to work the straight lines of Continental stitch.

Basket weave is started at the top-right-hand corner. It advances in diagonal rows, each row adding more stitches, and eventually fills in the entire shape or background. In working upward the needle is held horizontally (figure 2-45); in working downward the needle is held vertically (figure 2-46). Whether it is going up or down, the needle passes under two canvas threads, emerges in an empty hole, and is re-inserted diagonally upward to the right, over one canvas-thread intersection, in a hole already shared by another stitch. The work is never turned in starting another row.

Working two ascending or descending rows in succession should be avoided, since a faint ridge or line will be produced, which will show on the surface of the work. In working on regular mono canvas, if you remember that all descending rows should be worked over an intersection in which the vertical canvas thread is on top of the horizontal canvas thread, you will never have to worry about whether separate areas of stitching will join up correctly. Before it was discovered that working this way actually covered the canvas more completely, all backgrounds, once started, had to be worked continuously from the top-right-hand corner through the entire canvas to the lower-left-hand corner. The inability to stitch wherever desire dictated was the only detriment to basket-weave stitch, and it is now eliminated.

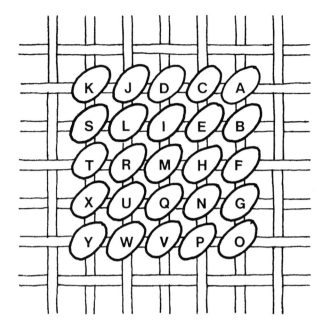

2-44.

2-45.

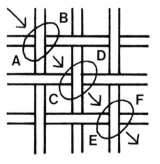

2-46.

If you continue to confuse your ups and downs—verticals and horizontals—mark a notation on the masking-tape binding of the canvas or memorize this wry question and answer: "V.D.? HA!" (vertical descending, horizontal ascending). If you cannot remember the formula or if you are working on interlock canvas, you will always have to start and finish your working thread in the middle of a row, never at the end, to enable you to keep track of whether you are working up or down. You should not jump to another place out of sequence.

To start or end threads in basket-weave stitch, always weave the threads under previously worked stitches on the back in a horizontal or vertical direction. End a thread in one direction and start the next thread in the other. Weaving them under diagonally will leave a ridge that will also show on the front.

Van Dyck Stitch

Van Dyck stitch (figure 2-47) gives a plaited or braid-like appearance. It is useful for stems and other lines, such as borders, and may also be used to fill leaf shapes—the center plait forms the central vein.

Bring the needle and thread out at A. Insert the needle diagonally upward to the right at B, take a tiny stitch to the left, and come out at C. Carry the thread over the distance from A to B and reinsert the needle at D on the same horizontal line as A. Carry the needle across the back and come out at E directly underneath A. Loop thread under the crossing of A to B and C to D from right to left—do not pierce the fabric—and reinsert the needle at F directly under D. Continue in this manner. Except for the first tiny stitch the back of the work will show only long horizontal stitches.

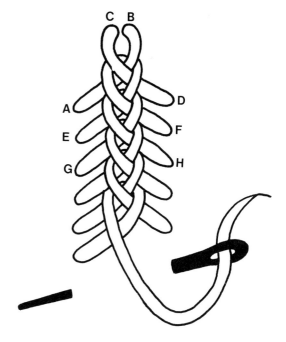

2-47.

TECHNIQUES
Designs on Canvas

There are two ways to follow a needlepoint design. One way is to buy a canvas with a design already painted on it and to match yarn colors to the colors chosen by some unknown artist. If red flowers were painted on the canvas, for example, they must be worked in red yarn. You may vary the color of red yarn by a couple of shades, but you must stay fairly close to the red shade painted. Using a yellow yarn on a red area would tend to distort the color, giving the yellow an orange cast. If you choose to work on a painted canvas,you must be absolutely sure that you like the colors.

The second way to follow a design gives you far more freedom. You work from a graphed design such as the ones in this book; each symbol on the graph represents a stitch in a certain color. Using a graph allows you to choose the finished dimensions of your project—you can work on any mesh of canvas you desire—and grants almost total freedom in color choice. Although specific colors are often indicated by a key to the symbols printed with the graph, you are completely at liberty to choose and stitch any colors you wish or even to delete design areas.

A clean, blank canvas also adds an element of surprise to the needlepoint, as each new stitch gives a more complete idea of what the finished work will look like. A needlepointer working from a graph is like an artist starting out with a blank canvas. Instead of covering the canvas with paint, the needlepointer covers it with yarn.

In working from a graphed design making a few marks on the canvas can help to speed the work along and to center the design properly, much like a painter's preliminary sketch. Great care must be taken, however, in choosing the medium for marking the canvas. Since most finished needlepoint must at some point be thoroughly dampened, the marker must be totally waterproof to prevent the colors from bleeding into the wool yarns and staining them.

Most commercially painted canvases are done with oils, and turpentine is used to thin the paint and clean the brushes. Because oils require a prolonged drying time and are rather messy to clean up, they should

not be your first choice.

Acrylic paints are just as accessible as oils. They are thinned with water at the time of use, and brushes can be cleaned with water while they are still wet. The drying time of the paints is quite short, and they are waterproof when dry. If you make a mistake on the canvas, you can wait until the paint is dry, cover it with white paint, and, after letting it dry, repaint it correctly. Because acrylics dry so quickly and are waterproof when dry, they are quite rough on brushes. You must be sure to keep your brushes wet at all times to prevent the paint from drying and ruining them. In applying paint keep it thin enough to apply clear color and not clog the canvas holes.

Oil-based felt-tipped markers are very handy to use and may even be carried around with your needlepoint for helpful marking whenever the need arises. I have had good success with these markers for many years, although they are more dangerous than either oils or acrylics. The problem lies not with the markers but with the sizing or starch used to stiffen the canvas. If the sizing is very thick or of bad quality, the marker color does not penetrate the canvas fibers but stays in the sizing. When the finished needlepoint is thoroughly dampened for blocking, the water may soften and move the sizing, along with the color, into the yarn.

If you want to use markers, test them on a small piece of canvas first. Let the colors dry overnight and then wash the test piece in warm water. If the colors bleed, use another type of canvas or another method of marking the canvas—or spray the marked canvas lightly with an acrylic fixative such as Krylon. The fixative ensures that your colors will never bleed onto the yarns and takes all the worry out of using markers.

Smell the markers you buy to be sure that they are actually oil-based. Most are marked "permanent," but they may not be. Magic Markers and Ad Markers are available in art-supply stores in over 120 colors, many with fine as well as broad points. Many needlework shops stock packages of six to eight markers developed especially for use on needlepoint canvas. Always test first, as you would for any marker.

Use your markers with a very light hand, as the color tends to spread somewhat. Mark only a very light spot on a single canvas thread or intersection of two threads. Do not use a marker in a darker color than your yarn, although you may use a slightly lighter shade.

I know of one needlepointer who stitched a good-sized 18-mesh canvas prepared with oil-based markers but without using acrylic fixative to lock in the colors. The canvas was thoroughly dampened and blocked with no problem. It was then mounted on a board for framing. Her husband decided to use a soil-repellent spray on the theory that if a little was good a lot was better. At that point, while they watched horrified, all the colors marked on the canvas began to bleed into the yarns! She eventually saved it by giving it numerous baths in lukewarm water, Woolite, and Ivory and rinses in running water. It cannot be overstressed that for absolute safety with markers the marked areas must be sprayed with acrylic fixative before stitching.

Designs on Fabric

In addition to the patterns given in this and other books you may find designs in other, sometimes unexpected places that cry out for embroidery. Unfortunately they are rarely the right size, and it may be necessary to enlarge or reduce them to the proper dimensions for your project.

To enlarge or reduce any design or line drawing to the exact size required for your embroidery, you can either photostat it to the exact dimensions or do the enlarging or reducing yourself at home. Photostating designs to the size required for curtains or other large projects can be very expensive, so it pays to learn the home method, even though it may take longer.

First trace the design onto plain tracing paper. Over this tracing superimpose a network of equal-sized squares. Pregraphed tracing paper is often available at art-supply stores. On another piece of tracing paper draw a rectangle the size desired and divide it into the same number of squares as the original tracing. Areas within individual squares on the original drawing that have a lot of detail may be further subdivided; subdivide the corresponding squares within the second frame. Draw the design freehand in the new frame square by square, faithfully repeating the lines and proportions of the original design (figure 2-48).

2-48.

There are several methods of transferring designs to fabric. Which one to use largely depends on the type of fabric you are working on. All the methods require tracing paper, tracing vellum, or architect's linen. The paper you use should not be as thin as tissue paper, for it must stand up to the abrasion of being written on at least twice, once over the bumpy surface of fabric.

The first method requires either carbon or graphite paper. Use either dressmakers' carbon, available in most fabric stores and notions departments, or graphite paper, available in art-supply stores. Graphite paper is preferable because it does not have a waxy surface, which can be inadvertently ironed permanently into the fabric. Do not use typewriter carbon because it will smudge. Tape or pin your fabric to a smooth, hard surface so that all the threads are straight. Pin the tracing-paper design to the fabric, centering the design. Homasote board covered with a sheet of poster board is a good working surface. You can use pushpins to keep your fabric and design securely in place. After your tracing is partly pinned down, slip a sheet of carbon or graphite paper between the tracing and the fabric, making sure the transferrable side is facing the fabric. For light-colored materials use a paper in the predominant color of your embroidery or a color dark enough to see clearly, such as blue, black, or red. For darker fabrics use yellow or white. Trace over the design on the tracing paper with a medium-hard pencil, pressing heavily enough so that the design is clearly transferred to the fabric below. You may lift one corner of the carbon paper to check your progress, but do not lift the whole design off the fabric until you are completely finished. Once the design paper is removed from the fabric, it is almost impossible to realign it perfectly.

Neither type of transfer paper is permanent (unless the dressmakers' carbon is ironed onto the fabric): it will wash out, making last-minute changes, corrections, and deletions in your design possible. Both types of transfer paper also tend to rub off with handling. If this happens, you will have to draw the design directly onto the fabric before the transferred lines become too faint to see. Use either watercolor and a fine brush, a fine-line washable (water-based) marker (test first for washability), pencil (it might smudge onto light-colored embroidery thread but will wash out), or a laundry-marking pen (it is indelible and will not wash out). Do not use a regular ball-point pen!

The second transfer method requires a hot-iron-transfer pencil. First trace your design onto tracing paper. Turn the tracing to the reverse side and retrace it with a special hot-iron-transfer pencil, either red or blue. Make sure to keep the point sharp, the lines thin, and the tracing free of smudges, because all lines will widen and all smudges will be transferred when the design is ironed on. It is important to remember that the transfer-pencil drawing must be in reverse to be reproduced correctly on the fabric. Pin, then baste the transfer drawing face down on the fabric, and press with a hot iron. Do not slide the iron around on the fabric—lift the iron to move it from area to area. It is a good idea to do a sample first on a corner or scrap of fabric to see how hot your iron should be to transfer the design properly without scorching the fabric. This method is very useful for transferring designs on large projects, but the lines produced on the fabric are absolutely permanent. Once the design is on the fabric, you cannot change your mind about the details. You must be absolutely sure that you are completely satisfied with the design before it is transferred. You must also be sure to cover the transferred design completely with stitches.

The third method requires a piece of cotton scrim. Use lightweight material such as batiste, organdy, or sheer muslin and transfer the design to it as though it were the actual embroidery fabric. A hot-iron-transfer pencil or a light box (described below) is the fastest way to transfer the design. Baste the scrim to the right side of the embroidery fabric and embroider through both layers. When all embroidery is finished, clip the scrim fairly close to the stitches but not close enough to endanger your stitching! With a pair of tweezers pull out the remaining scrim thread by thread. This is a time-consuming process but sometimes the only way to get a large design on a dark fabric. The skirt shown in figure 3-41 was embroidered in this way. This method has the added advantage of allowing you to change or move designs around, and it helps to keep the fabric clean while you are working. If you have pets or small children, this method is definitely recommended! The only disadvantage is that you cannot see how the design colors actually look on the colored fabric until the scrim is removed. But what a joyful surprise if you have chosen your colors correctly!

The last method requires a light box. Most people at one time or another have traced something by holding it up to a window so that light comes through from the reverse side. Many artists use a light box, a special box constructed with fluorescent lights beneath a piece of white plexiglass. To trace designs directly onto lightweight fabrics, you can make a temporary light box that is much easier on your arms and back than a window. Position a strong light to shine directly upwards under a fairly substantial piece of glass. A glass coffee table is ideal. Place your tracing on the glass and tape it down with masking tape. Tape the fabric over it and trace directly onto the fabric using a pencil, watercolor and a fine brush, or a fine-tip, washable marker.

Signing Your Work

No matter what technique you use to do your needlework, you will want to sign and date it. Try to include more than just your initials and the last two numbers of the year in which it was finished, for in fifty or a hundred years who will know who "Z.S.K." was or even in which "75" she finished her work! There is a great satisfaction in signing your work. Stitching in those letters and numbers means that the end of a long and enjoyable project is completed or nearly completed, and planning can begin on a new and equally stimulating piece of work.

A great deal of significant antique needlework is signed somewhere with the artist's full name and the place and date of completion. Even if this signature is hidden from public view in a seam allowance or under the frame of a chair, its presence adds uniqueness to the work and makes it more valuable both historically and intrinsically. If you can, plan to include more than just your initials somewhere in the piece.

To sign a piece of crewel, the easiest way is to write your signature, place, and date on a piece of paper in letters as large as you want them to appear on the embroidery. Using either the carbon-paper or light-box method, transfer them to the fabric. Use stem stitch, backstitch, or—my favorite—whipped backstitch.

Signing a piece of needlepoint or cross-stitch is a little more complicated than signing crewel. Lettering takes up an amazing amount of space in counted-thread embroidery, and specific plans for it, including graphing it out, must be made before the piece is stitched.

The first step in graphing lettering is to choose an alphabet. If you can see that your alloted space is very limited, choose the smallest alphabet you can find. Print the lettering out on paper, leaving some room between each letter. This is easier on graph paper. Count the number of stitches required for the width of each individual letter and mark the amount under the corresponding letter. Add one or two stitches apiece for the blank spaces between each letter and two or more blank spaces between each word. Do not forget commas and periods if there are any. Total the numbers on each individual line. For example, in the large alphabet shown in figure 2-49 the words "Stitched by" require at least 50 canvas threads in the width for needlepoint, 100 fabric threads for cross-stitch on linen fabric. The next step is to figure out how much space the line of lettering will take on your canvas or fabric. If you are working on 12-mesh canvas, that line will take a little over 4" (50 divided by 12). If you are working in cross-stitch on linen with 34 threads per inch—17 cross-stitches per inch—that line will take almost 3" (50 divided by 17). If your result is well within the limits of the space, measure the height of each line of lettering and add them together. To figure this dimension add the number of spaces below the line that letters such as g, p, q, and y will take plus at least one empty row between each line of lettering. In the example given above the total number of rows from the bottom of the y to the top of the S is 10; add 2 for the empty rows above and below to obtain a final total of 12. On 12-mesh canvas this would be the minimum number of canvas threads allowable. For three rows of lettering using this same alphabet 34 vertical threads would be the minimum.

Divide the total number of spaces for each line in half and determine the center of the printed lettering. Mark a centerline on the graph paper and copy the letters onto it, working from the center of each line toward either side. In stitching the lettering onto the fabric or canvas place the lines of letters symmetrically on either side of the center. Work as with the graphing—from the center toward either side—to ensure proper placement.

Washing, Pressing, and Blocking

If your needlepoint project is fairly large and has extensive areas of light or pale colors, it will probably need a light cleaning before blocking. Use a solution of mild soap such as Woolite and cool water. Dunk the needlepoint, swish it around, or knead it but do not scrub it. Rinse thoroughly in cool water. Never wring: roll the needlepoint in an absorbent towel, changing to a dry one when the first gets too wet to abosrb more water. Block immediately.

To block needlepoint, you will need a soft board larger on all sides than the entire piece of needlepoint. Plywood is good, but Homasote is better—the blocking pins go in quite easily and hold firmly. You will also need a sheet of brown wrapping paper on which to draw an outline of the outer dimensions of the needlepoint as you wish it to measure after blocking—neatly squared up. It is a good idea to do the drawing before you actually start stitching the needlepoint, since it will be out of shape when finished. You will also need tacks or pushpins. Rustless tacks, suggested by many authorities, are ideal, but pushpins are so easy to buy and use, even though they may rust, that I advocate using them. Since they do not go directly into the needlepoint, they can only deposit rust on the excess canvas, which you will probably be cutting off anyway.

2-49.

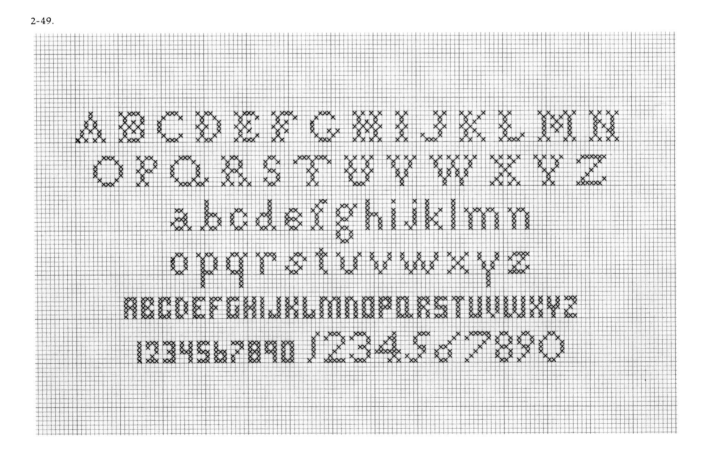

Tack or tape the paper to the board. Lay the needle-point on the board face down and begin pinning it through the paper to the board along one side, placing the pushpins at least 1" away from the needlepoint and ½" apart. If the pins are too close to the needle-point and too far apart, the edges of the stitched area will dry in an undesirable scallop pattern instead of being perfectly straight. Stretch the needle-point to exactly cover the outline drawn on the brown paper. Continue in this manner on the second side. At this point, if your needlepoint was not cleaned earlier, you will have to thoroughly wet it to enable you to stretch and pin down the third and fourth sides. Use a spray bottle for this—the kind used to mist houseplants. Use enough water to ensure that the piece is wet through. Finish pinning down the third and fourth sides and set the board aside to dry on a flat surface, away from the sun, for 24 to 48 hours.

When it is dry, remove the pushpins, and your needlepoint should be squared up and ready for mounting, but do not mount it yet, especially if it was badly distorted before blocking. Set the needle-point aside for a couple of days. In that time you should be able to see if it is going to crawl back out of shape again. If it does seem to be moving mysteri-ously back to its preblocking shape, block it again in exactly the same way as the first time. After it is dry but still on the blocking board, iron on some heavy-weight fusible, woven interfacing cut to fit the exact stitched area. This should help keep it in shape when you remove it from the board.

Like needlepoint, crewel embroidery will usually need a light cleaning when completed. Follow the same procedure. After it has been rolled in the towels to remove the excess moisture, either spread the work flat to dry (not in the sun) or press immediately while it is still damp.

To press, lay a single thickness of towel on your ironing board. Put your embroidery on the towel with the right side down. Dampen the piece if neces-sary with either a clean sponge or a spray bottle and iron lightly on the wrong side through a light-weight pressing cloth with a dry iron. I do not recom-mend the use of steam irons since they sometimes spit and leave stains. Be sure to use the proper setting on your iron for the fabric on which your embroidery

is worked. A preliminary test on a small scrap for proper heat setting is wise.

Embroidery that has drawn up and become puck-ered during working must be blocked instead of ironed. Follow the instructions given for blocking needlepoint, except that you must lay the work face up on the board so that the stitched areas stand out boldly. Make sure that all pins are beyond un-worked areas of fabric that are part of the finished product. If possible, all crewel embroidery should be blocked instead of ironed, for even though the soft towel placed under the embroidery on the ironing board permits the stitched areas to be raised above the fabric surface, they never stand out as boldly as on blocked pieces.

Mounting and Framing

Great care must be taken in both mounting and framing fine pieces of needlework. Remember too that you may eventually want to remove the needle-work from the frame and mounting for cleaning, so plan accordingly. Fine needlework is best mounted on artists' canvas-stretcher frames. These are avail-able in sections measured by 1" increments. For a piece of needlework 16" × 18", for example, you should buy two 16" lengths and two 18" lengths. These sections snap together easily without nails or screws. If your needlepoint measures 16½" × 18½", you can still mount it on 16"-×-18" stretchers, al-though a few rows of stitches would be hidden. A better procedure would be to add a few rows of stitching all around in the background color so that the piece would fit 17"-×-19" stretchers.

This problem does not arise with crewel em-broidery, since the background is the fabric itself and you presumably allowed generous margins be-fore you started work.

To mount a piece of needlepoint, lay it face down on a table. Place the assembled stretcher over it on the wrong side so that you can see only the last row of stitching around the outside edge of the stretcher. Temporarily tack the unworked-canvas margins to the narrow edges of the stretcher with pushpins, making sure that the needlework is stretched tightly and that all the lines of vertical and horizontal stitches are perfectly aligned. Using a staple gun and

¼" staples, permanently attach the canvas to the back of the stretcher (figure 2-50). Because of the thickness of the stretcher mitered corners cannot be done neatly. It is better to simply fold the sides one over the other at the corners. When the pushpins are removed, the needlepoint will be ready for framing.

In mounting crewel or other embroidery done on fabric rather than canvas, keeping the fabric threads perfectly aligned is more difficult. To make the job easier, weave a light sewing thread in a contrasting color around the perimeter of the work at the exact measurements of the stretcher, following a single fabric thread on each of the four sides. Because many embroidery fabrics are semitransparent, one or two layers of prewashed muslin or acid-free 100-percent-rag paper or matting board should be mounted on the stretcher underneath the embroidery. Follow the directions for mounting needlepoint, using the woven sewing thread as your guide for perfect alignment.

If at any time the needlework has to be removed from the stretcher, the staples can be pried out easily with either an awl or a small screwdriver. Although the staples may rust, they are at least 2" away from the stitched area and can do no harm.

2-50.

The back of the stretcher may be left as is or covered with a thin gray cardboard or muslin, either of which will allow needed moisture to pass through. The cardboard or muslin may be stapled or taped on.

After a careful study of pieces of fine needlework in museums, the Royal Academy of Needlework in England concluded that pieces that were not sealed between glass on the front and dustcovers on the back of the frames were in better condition than pieces that were so treated. The natural materials of needlework—wool, linen, cotton, and silk—need moisture to survive. Sealing needlework away from the air prevents its natural response to atmospheric changes and hastens its decay. I therefore do not recommend framing a piece of needlework destined to become an heirloom under glass. Of course, if you want to hang your needlework in the kitchen, where the normal accumulation of dust would eventually be glued to the stitched surface with cooking grease, framing behind regular glass—never the nonreflecting type—is essential. For needlework hung in other parts of the house, an occasional vacuuming of both the front and back is sufficient to keep it clean.

Although protective sprays such as Scotchgard are sometimes necessary for needlework that will receive hard wear, such as apparel and upholstery, they are unnecessary for framed pieces, since the plastic resins that cover the fibers repel needed moisture as well as soil.

Framing your needlework, once it is on a stretcher, is quite easy. Since it is mounted on a standard size, you may be able to simply walk into a framing store and buy a stock-size wooden frame, take it home, and insert the mounted needlework yourself, saving considerable expense. Wooden and polished- or painted-metal-strip frames are also available, which you can buy in four separate pieces and assemble at home with a few screws and metal angles, following the package directions.

Choosing the style of your frame is a matter of personal taste. Some people feel that a frame suitable to the period of the original needlework sould be used, while others prefer a simple modern frame, since, although the design of the needlework may be traditional, the actual stitching is contemporary.

Into every avid needleworker's life there comes a time when all the walls are covered with pictures

44

and guests start looking for places to drop pillows so that they may sit more comfortably on the couch! It is at this time that the needleworker starts looking for different kinds of projects. Pictures and pillows are safe, small, and not too expensive, so they are the projects that most people pick up quickly. But since needlework can be put to almost all the same uses as any fabric off the bolt, there is really no reason to limit yourself to the tried and true. A roomy purse worked in needlepoint or crewel will take no more time or money than two pillows; a slip seat for a chair will take almost the same amount of time and money as one pillow; and both those projects are far more functional than just another pillow. Of course you can make your pillows large enough to be upholstered as loose back cushions for your couch.

Rugs are large items involving a great deal of time and money, but the rewards of completing such projects far outweigh the drawbacks. In regard to the time element in making rugs it might be mentioned that the coverlet-patterned rug shown in figure 3-28 was completed in the space of 6 months, while at the same time I was stitching the Talish-patterned pillow shown in figure 3-30; designing, illustrating, and preparing all the other projects in this book; and keeping my home running more or less normally. Taking on such large projects really does not have to be as frightening as it seems to most people.

Buying the materials for large projects such as rugs, curtains, and upholstery can be expensive, but many needlework shops will hold your yarn for you and let you buy it as you need it, spreading the expense out over a longer period and at the same time assuring you of consistent dye lots. For a project such as the Talish rug shown in figure 3-31 consistent dyes are not required, since most of the original Caucasian and Oriental rugs were obviously made with numerous dye lots. This inconsistency of color is known as abrash and, since it seems to heighten the iridescence of the rug colors, is actually desired.

With each of the projects in this book I have included, in addition to complete instructions for finishing and making up or mounting each piece, suggestions for other uses of the individual designs.

3. DESIGNS

CREWEL BED HANGINGS

The most extravagant displays of the eighteenth-century crewelworker's art were sets of bed hangings. Few complete sets survive. Of those that do, perhaps the best known—and justifiably so—is the magnificent set worked by Mary Bulman of York, Maine, around 1745 (figure 3-1). The coverlet, curtains, and valances are supposed to have been stitched while her husband, Dr. Alexander Bulman, was serving as a surgeon at the siege of Louisbourg with Sir William Pepperell. His absence and subsequent death during the campaign may have inspired the rather melancholy verses on the valances. But the entire set, with its vivid hues and exuberant forms, is a celebration of life.

Mary Bulman worked in the English-derived-crewelwork tradition, basing her designs on tendrils and flowers. But she obviously stitched with great freedom. The flowers, leaves, and colors that she used are as fanciful as her imagination could make them.

3-1. Complete set of bed hangings by Mary Bulman, crewelwork on linen homespun, c. 1745. (Courtesy of the Old Gaol Museum, York, Maine.)

Surely they never grew in any garden. Although all the separate pieces of the set are clearly related, no two are exactly the same. Motifs are similar but do not actually repeat; sides and corners balance but are not identical. You, too, can work similar pieces freely, stressing motifs you like, eliminating others, or changing colors to suit your own taste. In adapting Mary Bulman's designs I have only presented the bare outlines of the motifs, leaving the choice of colors and stitches to your own fertile imagination.

The curtains shown in figure 3-2 were based on these designs, and over a hundred colors were used. Bj Hensley, who made the curtains, headed a group of women who stitched bedspread, window curtains, and bed hangings for the historic William Trent House in Trenton, N.J. and had a huge bag of leftover yarn to choose from for her own work. Even if you do not have a supply of leftover threads, you can still use many colors for your curtains without making a major investment in yarn, since single flowers and leaves take only one or two threads, and most yarn stores will sell by the thread as well as by the ounce or skein. Be sure that the fabric you choose for the curtains has a firm, tight weave and some linen content. After all your work you want the stitches to stay in place and not sag limply. Plan the yardage so that you can turn back large enough hems on the bottom and even on the sides to cover the entire stitched borders. Plan to line your curtains too to give some extra protection from the sun. Besides helping to preserve the curtains from fading and drying out, the lining will provide some extra insulation and give depth to the folds. Even with lining and extrawide hems it would be best to hang the curtains where they will not be exposed to direct sunlight for long periods.

3-2. Detail of curtains worked by Bj Hensley with designs adapted from the hangings shown in figure 3-1. (Photo by Ken Kaplowitz.)

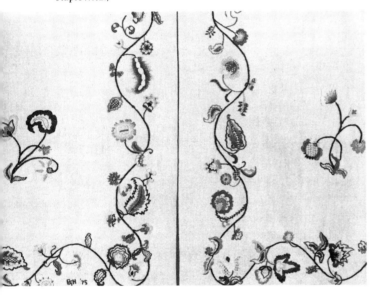

Crewel Curtains

It is a good idea to fix the rod that your curtains will be hung on in place before you measure for the yardage requirements. Measure from the top of the rod to either the sill, the bottom of the window apron, or the floor, depending on how long you want your curtains to be. To this measurement add enough for headings and bottom hems. How much to add depends on how you construct and hang the curtains. The total will tell you just how long to cut each window length. Be sure to cut the fabric straight by pulling out one thread from selvedge to selvedge and then cutting along that thread.

To measure where to cut your lining, keep in mind that it will be attached just below the heading at the top and that the bottom hem will overlap the top of the curtain hem by 1". Linings are usually cut to have a 2" hem at the bottom and ½" seams across the top and down either side. The embroidered horizontal and vertical borders for the right-hand (figure 3-3) and the left-hand (figure 3-4) curtains may be done directly on the curtains or, as an alternative to working on huge expanses of cloth, on narrow fabric panels that can be appliquéd to the curtains. With this method you can have the embroidery bands on different-colored fabric than the curtains themselves and can change the curtains whenever you want simply by removing the embroidered panels from one set of curtains and attaching them to another. The sprays scattered on the curtains (figures 3-5, 3-6, 3-7, 3-8, and 3-9) should be stitched directly on them, not on separate panels. Full-length curtains with appliquéd borders would also look beautiful if tiebacks were embroidered in parts of the border patterns but reduced in size. The scattered sprays could then be eliminated.

To begin, you must first decide on the length of the curtains and the width of the borders. The border motifs were designed to be enlarged to approximately 5½" in width; the continuing vine itself, 3½". At this width the designs will be 44" high and will fit easily across fabric measuring 45" to 54" from selvedge to selvedge. To make the designs taller to fit higher windows, continue the undulating vine, using flowers and leaves from the opposite curtain's *bottom* border to fill in. By changing the colors and stitches in these motifs, they will hardly resemble each other when finished. In making the designs taller notice that in the two border designs running up the centers there is a curvy motif opposite one with a sharp, jagged outline. Do not forget to end the vine neatly, turning it back on itself around the last flower. It is also possible to enlarge the designs so that the borders are wider than 5½".

Enlarge the designs for the borders to the size required by the graph-paper method described in chapter 2 or with a photostat. Transfer the designs to the fabric, making sure to leave room for hems at the bottom and sides and for headings at the top. Embroider the borders using crewel wools or Persian yarn in as many and as varied colors as you wish,

3-5.

3-6.

3-7.

3-8.

3-9.

3-3.

Right curtain horizontal border
Turn and match A to A on vertical border

3-4.

Left curtain horizontal border
Turn and match B to B on vertical border

filling some flowers and leaving others open, using the stitches described in this book and any others you prefer. Your palette may be vivid as in the Bulman bed hangings or soft as in the Hensley curtains. Keep the vine on which all the flowers and leaves grow a single color to help unify the myriad colors in the rest of the design. The smaller stems leading to the flowers and leaves may be in other colors. In stitching the second curtain panel keep in mind the colors that will be directly opposite in the first panel, especially those running up the center, since, when the curtains are closed, these colors will fall right next to each other.

When the borders are stitched, have someone hold the curtains up to the window as best they can to help you decide whether you want to add the five sprays scattered throughout the rest of the curtain. If you decide to stitch them, pin pieces of paper the approximate size of the enlarged sprays to the curtains to check the placement and the final size. Enlarge the sprays, transfer, and then stitch them.

Complementary valances may be added by running a portion of the border design in the width or by scattering three or four sprays across the top of the window.

When all the stitching is completed, wash the curtains if necessary and press them according to the directions in chapter 2. Be extremely careful because the high heat required to press linen can scorch the woolen embroidery threads. Blocking such large pieces of fabric would be impossible at home—have it done at your local dry cleaner's if necessary.

There are many different methods for constructing and hanging the stitched curtain panels—rod channels and loops for bare wooden rods; pleater tape or hand-stitched French pleats, box pleats, or cartridge pleats for traverse rods. How you decide to hang the curtains will depend upon the particular room setting and its use.

Suggestions for Other Uses

Think of everything you have ever seen stitched in crewel—chair seats, entire wing chairs, pocketbooks, bellpulls, framed pictures, and so on and on—you can stitch any of them using these designs as inspiration.

I am especially partial to the idea of stitching the border designs around the hem of a long skirt, using the sprays on patch pockets. Many museums have examples of eighteenth-century petticoats embroidered in much the same way. Imagine hiding all that fine stitching *under* your skirt!

BED RUG

Household inventories show that bed rugs were a common feature in early New England homes. Hooked or stitched on a heavy woolen backing, they provided comfort on cold nights. With central heating and electric blankets few of us would think of sleeping under anything as heavy as a bed rug. But their designs, simpler and more abstract than those found on upholsteries of the same period, appeal to modern eyes and can be adapted to many uses.

One common pattern can be found in a group of bed rugs from the New England area. Most of the known examples are initialed and dated in the first decade of the nineteenth century. The design of vines and carnations rising from a vase, however, harks back to the taste of the eighteenth century. Indeed, the pattern must have been known in that period as well, for at least two dated examples survive. One was worked in 1773 by Molly Stark, the wife of General John Stark, hero of the Battle of Bennington. The other, from which the design shown in figure 3-10 was taken, was stitched by Elizabeth Foot in 1778. Certainly the design harmonizes well with such eighteenth-century forms as the balloon seat of a Queen Anne or transitional chair.

Elizabeth Foot's bed rug is somewhat unusual in that it was worked predominantly in shades of blue. While blue and white was a favorite color scheme for coverlets and bed hangings, bed rugs were generally worked in warmer tones, perhaps to impart a visual impression of warmth. The design could easily be worked in any combination, polychrome or monochrome, realistic or fantastic, that complements your own color scheme. My adaptation of the Foot bed rug is 194 stitches wide by 215 stitches high. On 10-mesh canvas the finished measurements of the design area are 19 2/5" × 21 1/2"; on 12-mesh canvas, 16 1/10" × 17 9/10"; on 14-mesh canvas, 13 4/5" × 15 3/10".

3-10.

■ dark blue	321	⊡ light blue	355	□ background	153
◙ medium blue	323	⊠ brown	419		

Paterna Persian yarn numbers

3-11.

Framed Needlepoint

In planning this project, no matter which mesh canvas you choose, be sure to add at least 4" of unworked canvas for blocking and mounting and 2" of worked canvas in the background color. If you plan to sign the work at the bottom, as needlepointer Susan Bailey did, add 1" more to the length. For instance, 12-mesh canvas should be cut to measure no less than 22" × 25".

Bind the cut edges of the canvas with masking tape. Fold the canvas in half lengthwise and place a mark on the center canvas thread 4" from the bottom. This mark corresponds to the stitch marked by an arrow at the bottom of figure 3-10 and is the easiest place to start stitching. Before you actually start, count and transfer to the canvas the dark-blue vines and flower outlines in the chart, using an oil-based marker or acrylic paint in the same dark-blue color. The few hours this takes will save countless hours of stitching time.

First do all the dark-blue areas in Continental stitch. Then fill in the flowers with the other colors, using basket-weave stitch as much as possible. Graph and stitch your signature, then fill in the background using the basket-weave stitch throughout.

After the needlepoint is finished, block it and prepare it for mounting and framing according to the directions in chapter 2. A silver-metal frame, bought in the proper dimensions and screwed together in a few minutes, is an easy and attractive choice.

Suggestions for Other Uses

Because the type of design that Elizabeth Foot used for her bed rug can be seen in many pieces of eighteenth-century crewel embroidery, I have also included a line drawing of the design (figure 3-11) for the modern embroiderer.

Enlarge the design to the size desired following the directions in chapter 2 and transfer it to the fabric by one of the methods described earlier. If the fabric you choose is a twill or a tightly woven tabby, you may embroider freely using the crewel stitches described elsewhere in this book. If your fabric is the kind used for cross-stitch embroidery, with a fairly high thread count (32 per inch or more), you can darn the designs as Elizabeth Foot did—by weaving your threads in and out of the fabric in predetermined patterns. On the same kind of fabric the design can be worked from the needlepoint chart entirely in cross-stitch, leaving all background-color areas free of stitching. Whatever method you use, the completed needlework is admirably suited for use as a framed picture, a fire screen, or a chair-seat covering.

BARGELLO PURSE

Bargello, or flame stitch, generally describes canvas-work done with vertical stitches in contrast to the basically diagonal stitches of needlepoint. Although free embroidery was the most popular form in the eighteenth century, counted-thread work was also done, Bargello perhaps more frequently than needlepoint. Large-scale designs were used extensively for upholstery. Two notable wing chairs, one in the Metropolitan Museum of Art and another at Williamsburg, are worked in Bargello forms of the carnation pattern.

Very fine Bargello stitches were frequently used for articles of apparel. A favorite form was the clasped clutch purse. I based my shoulder-bag design on one of these, which is now in the Philadelphia Museum of Art. It was worked for George Grey in 1760. We can often get our best ideas of the original appearance of eighteenth-century needlework from such small surviving examples. Used rarely and carefully tucked away in a box or drawer, they have retained all their freshness of color. It was once thought that antique needlework was done in muted and faded tones. As more such pieces, which were always shielded from the effects of light and air, have been found, it becomes apparent that eighteenth-century taste favored brilliant, vivid hues and color combinations.

Bargello Shoulder Bag

This spectacular shoulder bag was worked by my mother, Zelda Kaman, in the Bargello four-two step on 16-mesh canvas using two plies of yarn in the needle. To make the same bag, you will need enough canvas to cut three pieces, each measuring 17" × 13½", for the back, front, and flap; and one piece, measuring 11" × 40", for the shoulder strap and boxing, which are worked side by side on the same

3-12.

■ black ◉ darkest ☒ dark ▽ medium • light ☐ lightest

54

piece. These measurements include seam allowances and unworked margins between the two long strips of needlework.

Bind the raw edges of the canvas pieces with masking tape to prevent the edges from raveling. Start with the three equal-sized pieces, keeping all stitching 2″ in from the canvas edges. The finished needlework will be approximately 9½″ × 13″. Work the black outlines for the carnation motifs (figure 3-12) first. Notice that the stitch count for the diagonal steps is not the same in all cases. From the bottom point to the outer edge the diagonal lines have eight, eight and seven stitches; from the outer edge to the top point the diagonal lines have eight, eight, and seven stitches.

After the black outlining for each piece is worked, fill in with the shaded colors following the diagrams of color-family placement for each motif in the front (figure 3-13), back (figure 3-14), and flap (figure 3-15) of the bag. From bottom to top the colors move from darker to lighter shades three times in each motif, and the topmost point is filled in with a few stitches of the second-to-darkest color in each family, as in the original. Notice that there are only three shades of yellow instead of the five that the other color families have. The lightest yellow is repeated three times. If you wish, you may use five shades of yellow. You can also change the entire color scheme—the bag would be just as beautiful in a monochromatic scheme, with all the motifs worked in shades of one color family.

The diagram for the front of the bag leaves a large triangular, unshaded section at the top for your complete signature, worked in tent stitch. Choose one of the darker yellows to stitch the lettering, then fill in the background with black tent stitch. You must use two plies in the needle for this area, although that much yarn is really too thick for 16-mesh canvas—one ply will not adequately cover it.

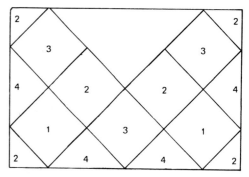

3-13.

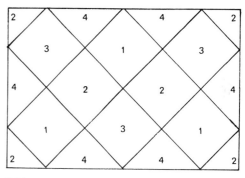

3-14.

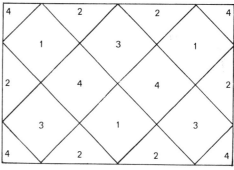

3-15.

Paterna Persian yarn numbers

black		050			
1. red	darkest	240	3. green	darkest	340
	dark	242		dark	367
	medium	843		medium	342
	light	852		light	352
	lightest	853		lightest	354
2. purple	darkest	610	4. yellow	darkest	427
	dark	612		medium	447
	medium	615		lightest	457
	light	618			
	lightest	620			

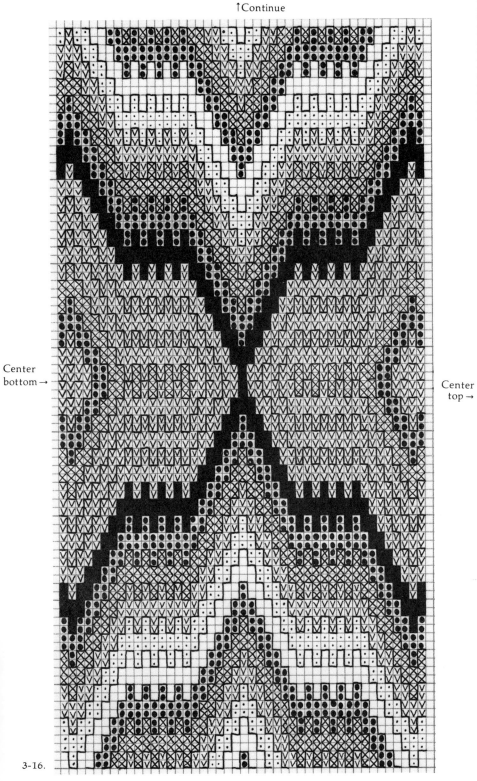

Center
bottom →

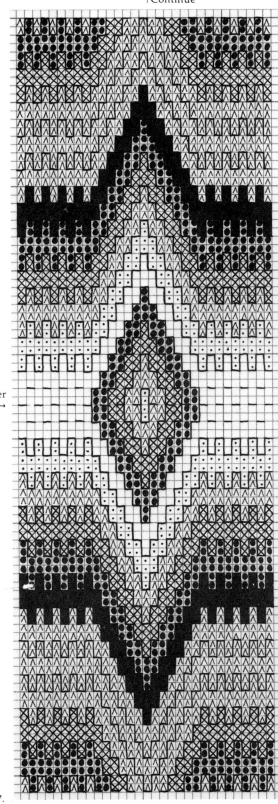

Center
top →

3-16.

3-17.

To work the boxing strip (figure 3-16) and the shoulder strap (figure 3-17), fold the long piece of canvas in half across the width and mark the two center threads. Leave a 2" margin on the outer edges and between the two pieces of needlework. Do not cut them apart until the blocking is finished and you are ready to start making up the bag. Follow the individual charts and stitch the two pieces side by side, working symmetrically outwards from the center. For the shoulder strap the purples will be in the center as charted, followed by 15 rows each of the yellows, reds, greens, and purples; each family is shaded three times from dark to light, with one row of black separating the families. End with the black row and fill in the two sides of the point with yellow. For the boxing two halves of yellow motifs are centered, followed by 15 rows each of purple, green, red, and yellow, again with each color family separated by one row of black. The shoulder strap will be approximately 2" × 36"; the boxing strip, 3" × 33".

The symbols on the charts (except for the black) do not refer to specific colors but to shades within the color families from dark to light. Each group of four symbols, aligned vertically on the chart, represents one vertical stitch taken over four horizontal canvas threads.

Construction

Cut the excess canvas from all worked pieces, allowing a 1¼" edge for the seam allowance. Zigzag the raw edges on a sewing machine or overcast them by hand.

Cut a piece of woven iron-on interfacing the exact size of the worked flap and press it to the underside. Preshrink 1"-wide twill tape or satin ribbon, then cut a piece as long as the front flap. Place the tape ¼" from the bottom edge of the front-flap seam allowance, topstitch it on close to the edge on three sides, and slide in a metal corset stay approximately ⅝" wide. Corset stays can be bought or ordered from button, sewing, notion, or specialty shops and are available in various lengths and widths. Metal stays are impossible to cut to the proper length at home but are the best. Whalebone stays can be cut at home but are more liable to break with use. They can sometimes be found in old corsets at rummage sales and thrift shops. If you cannot find corset stays, the best alternative is to cut strips from plastic milk bottles.

Stitch down the fourth side of the tape. Fold the seam allowance over the stay and baste lightly to the interfacing, making sure that no canvas threads show on the edge. Lightly press, using a pressing cloth and steam. Miter all four corners, fold the remaining three seam allowances under, and baste to the interfacing. Do not allow any canvas threads to show. Press on another interfacing layer, covering the seam allowances.

Cut a piece of interfacing the same size as the worked front and press it to the underside. Place tape ¼" from the top-edge seam allowance, topstitch it on close to the edge on three sides, and slide in the stay. Then stitch down the fourth side of the tape. Fold the seam allowance over the stay and baste lightly to the interfacing, making sure that no canvas threads show on the edge. Miter all four corners, fold the remaining three seam allowances under, and baste lightly to the interfacing, allowing one canvas thread to show on the edge. Press on another interfacing layer, covering the seam allowances.

Cut a piece of interfacing the same size as the worked back and press it to the underside. Miter all four corners, fold the four seam allowances, and baste them lightly to the interfacing, leaving one canvas thread showing on the bottom and on two sides but not on the top. Press on another interfacing, covering the seam allowances.

Cut a piece of interfacing the exact size as the worked piece of boxing and press it on the underside. Lightly glue a piece of cardboard 2½" × 12½" to the exact center of the boxing strip. Weight it down with books or magazines until dry, then insert four brass nailhead-type feet (available at notions counters) on the right side, 2" in from the sides of the cardboard. Fold under the seam allowances on both long sides, leaving one canvas thread showing on the edge, and glue them to the cardboard, basting them to the interfacing where the cardboard ends. Leave the edge loose 1½" from each end. Press. Cut another piece of interfacing 2½" × 12½" and press it on top of the cardboard, covering the seam allowances.

Cut a piece of interfacing the exact size of the worked piece of shoulder strap. Press it on. Miter all four corners, fold back the seam allowance plus two worked threads, and baste them to the interfacing. Cut a second piece of interfacing to cover all the canvas on the back of the shoulder strap, being careful not to cover the two worked threads that were turned back. Press it on.

Cut a piece of lining the size of the front plus 2″ for seam allowances. Press under the 1″ seam allowances, mitering all four corners. Baste the lining to the underside of the front. Hand-stitch close to the edge on the top part. Hand-stitch onto the remaining three sides, leaving one canvas thread showing on the edge.

Cut a piece of lining the size of the flap plus 2″ for seam allowances. Press under the 1″ seam allowances, mitering all four corners. Baste the lining to the underside of the flap. Hand-stitch close to the edge on all four sides. Pin the top of the lined front flap on top of the unlined back piece, overlapping them 2⅛″, and topstitch ⅛″ from the overlapped edge on a sewing machine. Stitch again over the first line of stitching. Steam-press lightly.

Cut a piece of lining the size of the back plus 2″ for seam allowances. If you wish, you can add a small compartment for a wallet or mirror by cutting a piece of lining material twice the desired size plus seam allowances. Press a piece of interfacing to the underside of the pocket. Fold it in half, right sides together, and sew on the seam allowance on two sides. Turn to the right side and press. Fold in the seam allowance on the remaining side and place the pocket about 1½″ from the bottom of the lining. Stitch it down by machine on three sides. Press under the 1″ seam allowances of the lining, mitering all four corners. Making sure that the pocket compartment is placed in the proper position, baste the lining to the underside of the back piece. Hand-stitch close to the top edge, then onto the remaining three sides, leaving one canvas thread showing.

Cut a piece of lining the size of the boxing plus 2″ for seam allowances. Press under the 1″ seam allowance on the two long edges. Baste the lining to the boxing. Hand-stitch on the two long sides, leaving one canvas thread showing.

Cut a piece of lining the size of the shoulder strap plus 2″ for seam allowances. Press under the 1″ seam allowance on all four sides, mitering the corners. Baste the lining to the shoulder strap. Hand-stitch close to the edges on the short sides, next to the two

worked threads on the long sides.

Matching the bottom center of the boxing to the bottom-center edge of the front piece and with the wrong (lined) sides facing, start at the center bottom and hand-stitch the two pieces together with the binding stitch, using two strands of black wool yarn and matching opposite canvas threads on each piece. Fold in the excess boxing and boxing lining on the top and blindstitch in place. Repeat from the center to the other side. Press lightly.

To attach the shoulder strap to the boxing, place the strap on top, matching the designs, and either top stitch ⅛″ from the edge by machine or overcast securely with a double strand of black wool yarn.

Attach the bottom of the back piece to the other edge of the boxing in the same manner as for the front, making sure to leave the flap free.

Make a yarn buttonhole loop by sewing several strands of yarn to the center bottom of the flap; the loop should be about 2″ long. Then work buttonhole stitches over the strands, packing them tightly. Sew a ¾″ black mat-finish ball button to the center front ½″ below the signature section.

Sling the bag over your shoulder, leave the house, and take a walk downtown!

Suggestions for Other Uses

Because the carnation motif used on the shoulder bag is rather large in comparison to other Bargello patterns, its use is limited to rather large articles. It is further limited by the fact that it is a one-way design. It would be suitable for tie-on pads for chair seats and backs, for covering cylindrical wastebaskets, and for cushions and pillows.

If you are looking for a really important project, think about using this pattern to upholster an entire wing chair. A number of museums have chairs covered completely in flame stitch or Bargello, which you should see for inspiration and reassurance. Have an upholsterer make muslin patterns of your chair before you start. If you buy a modern reproduction of a wing chair, you may be able to get paper upholstery patterns from the manufacturer—as I did—simply by requesting them.

CHINESE EXPORT PLATE

For centuries porcelain making was a Chinese secret. So famous was their output that the word "china" became synonymous with the finest products of the potter's art. Even before the American Revolution some Chinese wares adorned the wealthiest homes. After direct American trade with China was opened in the 1780s, Chinese porcelains became almost ubiquitous and remained in favor until English wares became fashionable in the 1830s and '40s.

Much Chinese porcelain can still be found in antique shops, ranging from the relatively coarse blue-and-white Canton pattern to heraldic pieces or delicate floral patterns like the one shown in figure 3-18. While the blue on white, sometimes combined with red, is the most common color scheme, monochrome decoration in orange or, more rarely, green may also be found, as well as polychrome decoration.

The delicate motifs used on export porcelain in the late eighteenth and early nineteenth centuries go well with the Hepplewhite and Sheraton furniture of the period or with later pieces reflecting the taste of that era. The floral pattern was adapted to a needlepoint chair seat and mounted on a Centennial Hepplewhite chair. Your own china pattern, whatever period it is from, can also serve as a source for upholstery or cushions for dining-room chairs. Usually the design will have to be simplified. In this particular plate, for example, I omitted one of the borders. Had the main design been bolder and less diffuse, the rim might have been dispensed with altogether. For instructions on how to trace your own pattern, size it, and transfer it to canvas, see the suggestions at the end of the project.

My graph, based on an eighteenth-century polychrome Chinese Export plate (figure 3-18), specifies yarn colors as close to the original plate as I could find. If the blues do not suit your dining room, they can be changed easily to greens or even browns. The colors of the flowers would suit most color schemes. Worked on 14-mesh canvas, this circular design will measure about 10½"; on 12-mesh canvas, 12½"; and on 10-mesh canvas, just over 15".

This design was stitched specifically for an upholstered chair but will work equally well as a covering for a slip-seat chair or even as a tie-on cushion for a wood, cane, or rush chair seat.

Needlepoint Chair Seat

Before preparing your canvas, you must make a pattern so that the finished needlepoint actually fits the chair it is being made for. If your chair does not need reupholstery but just a new covering, it may be possible to remove the old fabric carefully and use it as the pattern for your needlepoint. If your chair is to be reupholstered or if removing the old fabric is impossible at this time, you must make a cloth pattern yourself. To do this, use muslin or an old sheet. Lay it on the seat and pin it around all the edges, making soft, even pleats in the corners where it drops down the sides. Cut off the excess fabric where the chair back, arms, and legs alter the regular shape of the seat. When the cloth pattern is taken off the chair, it should be folded in half from front to back and pressed along the fold. Check while it is folded to make sure that the two sides are exactly the same. Mark the exact center of the cloth pattern.

The canvas that you work on should be rectangular, no matter what the shape of the seat is, and at least 4" larger than the pattern in each direction. Bind the edges of the canvas with masking tape to prevent them from raveling. Lay the folded cloth pattern on the canvas, making sure to align the fold along a single canvas thread running from top to bottom, and mark this canvas thread. Open out the fold and pin the entire cloth pattern to the canvas. Then mark the outline of the pattern onto the canvas, allowing 1" beyond it all the way around. Mark the center of the pattern onto the canvas.

Most upholsterers prefer to work with needlepoint that is stitched even in the areas that will eventually be cut away, such as where the back of the chair joins the seat. Making your canvas pattern at least a generous inch larger than the cloth pattern should give any upholsterer (yourself?) plenty of needlepoint with which to work.

Center and stitch the design from the graph in figure 3-18, beginning with the inner blue circle. Find the stems in the floral motifs that are easiest to count to from that stitched circle and work them. Finish each isolated floral motif before moving to the next. If you wish, you may overstitch the areas indicated as "white 005" with silk or cotton to add a shiny highlight or two.

3-18.

Paterna Persian yarn numbers

- ■ dark blue 323
- medium blue 355
- dark rose 236
- medium rose 282
- light rose 288
- dark yellow-green 545
- medium yellow-green 550
- light yellow-green 580
- dark orange 424
- medium orange 444
- ☒ bright green 510
- dark green 505
- white 005
- □ background 017

If in moving from one isolated motif to the next you find that you have miscounted by one or two threads, do not worry. As long as the motifs do not touch or come too close to the inner circle, the designs will look fine. Only after the center of the design, including the background color, is worked should you complete the design in the circular rim. If those stitches were worked first, they might get too roughed up by handling.

When the design area is stitched, fill in the background. If you plan to work a number of chair seats, it is wise to choose a fast-moving background stitch. Working such large areas in tent stitch in a single color may prove very boring very quickly, and you may find yourself losing interest in the whole project. Constance Greiff, who made the piece shown here, used tent stitch for the design area and mosaic stitch for the background outside the circle.

When all the stitching is completed, clean the needlepoint if necessary and block it.

Covering the Chair

Set the chair up on a table or on sawhorses so you can work comfortably. Remove the old covering. If the chair is an antique, you may find that some of the tacks have been driven below the surface of the wood. Do not try to remove those tacks, because it would chew up the old, dry wood even more. Just leave them where they are and work around them.

Replace the old cotton batting with new batting, dropping it down the sides but making sure that it does not cover the area where you will be tacking (figure 3-19). Tear the batting to the proper size, using one hand as a straightedge to tear against.

Measure and lightly mark the centers of all four sides of the needlepoint and the chair seat with a piece of chalk.

Lay the needlepoint on the seat and, using size-3 or -4 upholsterers' tacks, temporarily tack the center of each side to the seat, making sure that the design is centered. On chairs that are viewed primarily from the front place the design slightly in front of the center of the seat. Be sure to keep the grain of the needlepoint running straight from front to back and side to side. If the wood is very old and full of tack holes, you may have to use size-5 or -6 tacks for

better hold. Pushpins can be used for temporary tacking; staples in a staple gun, for permanent tacking.

Temporarily tack the front and sides to within 2" of each corner, moving the tacks until you are sure that the lines are straight and that the needlepoint is stretched tightly enough. As you tack, pull the excess towards the corners.

Fold the back section of needlepoint forward over the chair and cut the canvas diagonally from the corners to within ¼" of where the needlepoint meets the back posts of the chair (figure 3-20). This is scary! Cut too little at first and, if it is not enough, take another little nip.

3-19.

3-20.

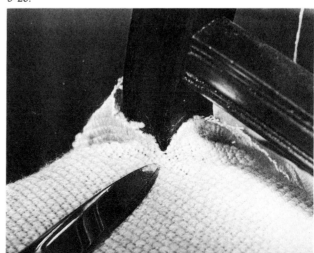

Fold the needlepoint down between the posts to the back. On the straight of the canvas cut away all but 1" of excess needlepoint on either side of each post (figure 3-21). All the excess will be folded under and tucked in. Make your cuts by trial and error. Cut too little at first, then fold to see if the needlepoint will fit neatly between the posts without wrinkling. If it seems to wrinkle and does not lie smoothly, make another little nip, fold, and check again. Pick out one row of stitches and follow it between the posts to make sure that the grain is straight. Press the folds flat by lightly tapping with a hammer.

When you are sure that the placement is perfect and there are no wrinkles, start putting in the permanent tacks. Do the back and sides first, working to within 2" of the front corners and placing the tacks ¾" to 1" apart. Tack the front to within 2" of the corners. On curved edges ease in the slight fullness between tacks and place the tacks closer together.

The pleats made to fold away the excess needlepoint on the front corners are placed on the front of the seat so that the fold openings can only be seen from the sides. Smoothing the excess needlepoint down and towards the corners from the top along the grain of the needlepoint, pull the excess from the side around to the front and tack it on the edge of the front (figure 3-22). These tacks will be covered by the rest of the pleat.

Cut off the excess needlepoint in the folded underside of the pleat (figure 3-23). The cuts are made so that the corners will not be too bulky when the pleat is finally folded and tacked. Fold the pleat slightly short of the corner and pull it to the corner for a sharp edge (figure 3-24). Use a nail file to push in the fold of the pleat and to keep the edges sharp and straight. Press the fold flat by lightly tapping it with a hammer. Tack the pleated corner, placing the tacks ¼" apart. After the pleat is folded and tacked, the fold opening can be closed invisibly with a curved needle and light thread.

Using a *very* sharp knife or blade, cut away the excess needlepoint below the tacks (figure 3-25). If you hit a tack while cutting, you will probably dull your edge, so keep a sharpener handy.

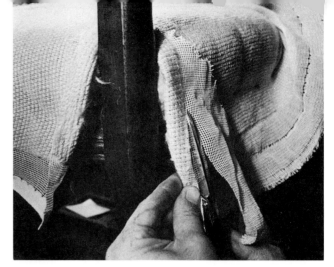

3-21.

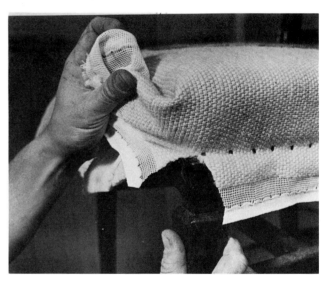

3-22.

3-23.

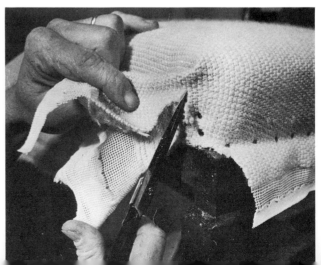

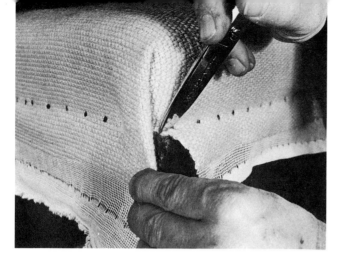

3-24.

To cover the tacks, use store-bought gimp or decorative braid in a matching or contrasting color. Tuck in the starting edge at a corner and temporarily tack it in place. Brush white glue onto the wrong side of the gimp and place it around the chair to hide the cut edge of the needlepoint and the tacks (figure 3-26). Tuck each starting edge under at the corners and tack temporarily in place. Press the gimp into proper position by lightly tapping it with a hammer. Tack temporarily wherever needed until the glue is set, two hours at the most. To remove the temporary tacks, twist them first to break the bond before pulling them straight out. Figure 3-27 shows the completed seat in place on the chair.

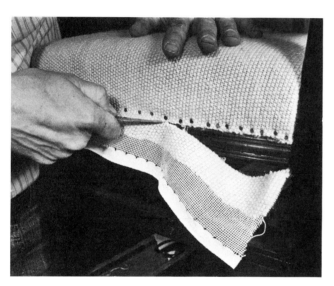

3-25.

3-26.

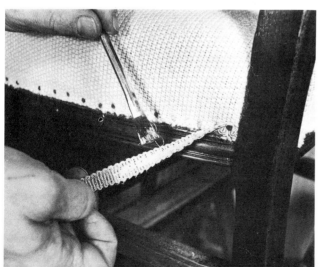

3-27.

Suggestions for Other Uses

Any of the small floral sprays may be lifted from the design, rearranged, and used on small articles such as clutch bags. The outer circular frame may be used alone to frame pictures. Worked on 10-mesh canvas, the entire design as charted would make a 15″ round pillow.

It is hoped that this design will inspire you to graph and stitch chair seats based on your own china patterns. First decide what mesh canvas you want to stitch. Then decide how large you want the design to appear on the chair. An easy way to determine this is by laying plates of different sizes on the chair until you find one that fits nicely in the seat area. After you have decided how large your design will be, figure out how many meshes it will require on your canvas by multiplying the number of meshes per inch by the size of the design. A 10″ design will take 140 meshes on 14-mesh canvas; 120 meshes, on 12-mesh canvas.

If you have planned a 10″ design on 14-mesh canvas, for example, mark an area 140 squares by 140 squares on graph paper. The most common graph paper has 10 squares per inch; the graphed design on this paper will be larger than the stitched design. This disparity of size is of no consequence. Once the design is charted on the graph paper and if each square is carefully reproduced on the canvas as one tent stitch, the design will be a stitched version of the graph in the exact size desired.

Trace the design directly from the plate and enlarge it to fit within the blocked-out graph-paper area by the squares method explained in chapter 2 or by photostating it. Trace the enlarged design onto the graph paper and step the curved lines of each color area along the squares. Indicate the color areas by using different symbols for each color or with colored pencils. Remember that, to be effective as stitchery, many details and subtle curves must be deleted from the original, although the larger the graphed design is (that is, the greater the number of stitches in each design), the more details and subtle curves may be added. When you buy your yarn, take your plate with you so you can match the colors exactly.

If your chairs are made entirely of wood or have cane seats, you can make tie-on cushions with your needlepoint. Five of my own tie-on chair cushions are now completed, stitched in the Meissen blue-onion pattern, the antique china I collect. These are made exactly like boxed pillows except that the fillers are single slabs of 1″ foam rubber cut to size with an electric carving knife.

TALISH RUG

The fashion for rugs from the Near East has been a recurrent theme in American interior decoration. They have always been something of a luxury, enjoyed for their rarity as well as for their beauty. We know of the pride wealthy Americans in the eighteenth century took in such possessions from portraits in which rugs are portrayed fairly frequently. However, their luxury status is attested to by their rare appearance as floor coverings. Large carpets must have been very costly indeed; what are shown are generally small rugs, used in the Dutch fashion as table coverings.

Replaced in fashion by various kinds of carpeting, oriental rugs became popular again in the third quarter of the nineteenth century; they were woven both in traditional patterns and in designs developed for the western market. By this time large room-size rugs and runners were imported, as well as the smaller scatter rugs. The 1920s and the 1960s are other periods in which oriental rugs inspired an almost cultlike admiration. It is a fervor which is well deserved. The intricate stylized patterns and subtle color schemes complement furnishings of every period from Queen Anne to contemporary.

I based my design for a large pillow on an early nineteenth-century Talish rug (figure 3-28). Talish rugs, woven in a mountainous area near the Caspian Sea, are generally found in the form of fairly small runners, with a width of just over 3′ and a length up to 7′ or 8′. They usually have a plain-blue center field, edged with a reciprocating arrowhead motif, but in some the field is filled with stars or sometimes with tulips. Most characteristic is a wide inner border with rosettes centered between groups of broken squares or star shapes on a white field. This border is flanked by smaller borders of squares or stars in many alternating colors with a reciprocating trefoil-patterned outer border.

Needlepoint Pillow

Graphing the Talish rug for needlepoint was fairly easy and took very little time because of the pattern repeats. Geometrically patterned Caucasian rugs in your own home may provide inspiration for your original needlepoint. First turn the rug to the wrong side, where it is usually easier to see each individual knot. Count the knots color by color, knot by knot, and indicate them on graph paper by color symbols. You may have to reduce each individual motif to make the overall size of the pillow manageable and then make a new chart (figure 3-29), as I did for the Talish.

The colors used in the original Talish rug can be matched exactly to the colors in the Paterna Persian-yarn range. It is easy to match rug colors with yarns, especially so for any design derived from an oriental rug, because, as mentioned earlier, the Paternayan colors were originally developed to repair and even to make new oriental rugs.

3-29.

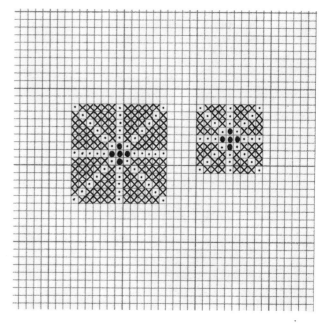

3-28. Talish rug (92″ × 42″) from the early nineteenth century, wool and cotton, with 110 Ghiordes knots per square inch. (Courtesy of Mr. and Mrs. Bruce Westcott.)

The chart for the Talish rug design (figure 3-30) is 271 stitches square. On 14-mesh canvas a pillow worked in this design will measure about 19″. The canvas should measure at least 24″ square to allow extra material for blocking and seam allowances. Bind the cut edges with masking tape to prevent the canvas threads from unraveling as you work.

With a light-blue shade of either acrylic paint or marking pen draw a square on the canvas that measures 271 threads in each direction, starting at least 2″ in from one corner. This line defines the outermost boundary of stitching and corresponds to the outermost line of Xs on the graph. If you count and mark on the canvas the other single lines of light-blue stitching that outline the various borders of the design, your work will be much easier, for you will not have to do as much piecemeal counting while you stitch. If you do your marking with a marking pen, do not forget to spray the areas with acrylic fixative.

Use two strands of Paterna Persian yarn in the needle for 14-mesh canvas in the colors indicated. Start your stitching in the large center square, working the red outline of the reversing-arrowhead motifs surrounding it first. Then fill in the dark blue of the center. The dark square in the center of the open blue field on the graph indicates the center stitch in the entire design and is, of course, also to be done in dark blue. After the blue field is done, start working around it, doing each successive border as it appears in the chart. Work the Continental stitch for single long lines of color and keep your stitches fairly loose so as not to pull the canvas badly out of shape. Much of the rest of the design can be done in the basket-weave stitch.

Although the motifs in the two matching red border designs contain many subtle variations in the arrangement of the colors, the colors do repeat often enough so that you can usually carry a color from one motif to the next and to the next—you won't have to start and end threads as often as it might seem. Note in these borders that while most of the small motifs are separated by *four* rows of red, the two motifs on either side of the centerline (the 136th canvas thread) are separated by only *three* rows.

Although the design ends with a single line of light blue, it is suggested that you stitch at least four more rows in the same color around the entire design.

There are a couple of reasons for this. The first is that when you sew your cushion together, it is better to sew between two stitched rows than between a stitched row and blank canvas—the canvas might peek through the stitching. The second reason is that the bias cording used to edge the pillow tends to roll forward, obscuring the last row or two of stitching. The last row is as important to the overall design as all the other rows, and adding three more rows before you sew the pillow together will ensure that the last design row will be visible. When all your stitching is complete, block the needlepoint according to the directions given in chapter 2.

If you are searching for a fabric to back the pillow, take the needlepoint with you and keep your mind open. Thinking that a dark-blue upholstery plush was in order, I went to about seven stores with no luck, but in the eighth store the manager told me he had something in the basement that would be right. Even in the poor light I could see that the bolt of deep brick-red suedecloth he pulled out was the only choice I could have made. It matched the red of the design perfectly!

Making The Pillow

To make self-cording of the backing material, measure 2″-wide true-bias strips of heavy upholstery fabric or Ultrasuede. Cut and sew the strips together to equal the finished perimeter of the pillow plus 2″ more than the total length. For machine sewing use a heavy-duty needle and heavier thread than you would normally use. Steam-press the seams open or glue down with a thin layer of school paste, which washes out. Lay the strip on the floor wrong side up. Run a thin line of glue down the exact middle of the strip. Lay the cording along the glue line and place a few magazines on top to keep the cording in place until dry. In a few hours when it is dry, starting at one end of the strip, fold it in half over the cording and pinch it together with a spring-type paper clip. Using the zipper-foot attachment, machine-sew along the length of cording, sliding the clip forward every few inches to keep the fold in place.

Machine-zigzag twice around the unworked canvas ¾″ away from the worked area. Cut the excess canvas close to the machine stitching. Put the finished bias

Center →

3-30.   Paterna Persian yarn numbers

⊡ white 513	⊠ light blue 330
⊙ red 240	⊻ blue-green 367
◪ black 050	⊔ purple 117
⊞ dark blue 334	⊘ gold 453

Center

Color sequences on pages 68–69.

Color sequence of small motifs in inner red border.

Centers	Lines	Triangles			
1. gold	red	blue-green	19. light blue	black	gold
2. blue-green	black	white	20. gold	red	black
3. light blue	red	black	21. red	black	white
4. red	black	gold	22. white	red	blue-green
5. red	gold	black	23. white	blue-green	purple
6. black	red	light blue	24. blue-green	black	gold
7. blue-green	gold	purple	25. white	red	dark blue
8. white	red	dark blue	26. gold	dark blue	white
9. light blue	red	blue-green	27. black	red	blue-green
10. gold	blue-green	black	28. gold	blue-green	purple
11. blue-green	black	gold	29. red	black	gold
12. white	blue-green	purple	30. blue-green	gold	black
13. blue-green	purple	gold	31. dark blue	red	light blue
14. gold	red	black	32. light blue	black	gold
15. blue-green	black	white	33. blue-green	dark blue	purple
16. white	red	blue-green	34. black	red	blue-green
17. black	gold	purple	35. red	blue-green	white
18. black	red	light blue	36. black	gold	dark blue

Color sequence of large motifs in white main border.

Outlines	Outer diamonds and squares	Center diamond	Other diamonds	Hooks	Background
1. black	gold	red	red	light blue	purple
2. red	blue-green	white	white	gold	dark blue
3. black	blue-green	blue-green	gold	light blue	red
4. red	light blue	light blue	white	purple	dark blue
5. blue-green	red	white	red	dark blue	purple
6. red	light blue	gold	black	gold	blue-green
7. black	light blue	white	gold	blue-green	red
8. red	dark blue	gold	black	gold	light blue
9. dark blue	purple	gold	white	light blue	red
10. black	blue-green	red	gold	light blue	purple
11. blue-green	gold	gold	red	white	dark blue
12. red	black	gold	gold	dark blue	blue-green

Color sequence of small motifs in outer red border.

Centers	Lines	Triangles		Centers	Lines	Triangles
1. dark blue	black	gold	35. red	gold	black
2. gold	dark blue	purple	36. black	red	light blue
3. black	gold	blue-green	37. blue-green	gold	purple
4. blue-green	red	black	38. white	red	dark blue
5. gold	red	dark blue	39. gold	blue-green	black
6. blue-green	black	gold	40. light blue	red	blue-green
7. gold	dark blue	purple	41. blue-green	black	gold
8. red	blue-green	light blue	42. white	blue-green	purple
9. black	red	blue-green	43. blue-green	purple	gold
10. dark blue	gold	purple	44. gold	red	black
11. black	red	light blue	45. blue-green	black	white
12. white	dark blue	gold	46. white	red	blue-green
13. light blue	red	black	47. black	gold	purple
14. red	dark blue	white	48. black	red	dark blue
15. black	red	light blue	49. dark blue	black	gold
16. blue-green	gold	black	50. gold	red	black
17. gold	blue-green	purple	51. red	black	white
18. gold	red	blue-green	52. white	red	blue-green
19. black	light blue	gold	53. dark blue	black	gold
20. white	red	blue-green	54. white	blue-green	purple
21. gold	dark blue	white	55. red	gold	blue-green
22. red	white	black	56. blue-green	black	gold
23. gold	blue-green	purple	57. white	purple	dark blue
24. red	dark blue	gold	58. gold	dark blue	light blue
25. red	blue-green	dark blue	59. black	red	blue-green
26. black	gold	blue-green	60. gold	blue-green	purple
27. white	dark blue	purple	61. red	black	gold
28. dark blue	red	white	62. dark blue	red	purple
29. gold	light blue	black	63. blue-green	gold	black
30. red	light blue	gold	64. dark blue	red	light blue
31. gold	red	blue-green	65. light blue	black	gold
32. blue-green	black	white	66. white	blue-green	purple
33. light blue	red	black	67. black	red	blue-green
34. red	black	gold	68. red	dark blue	white

69

cording down on the front of the needlepoint, folded edge on the work, cut edge on the unworked canvas. Hand-stitch the cording to the needlepoint, with the stitching line inside the last worked row. At each corner clip the seam allowance of the cording just at the machine stitching, taking care not to cut the stitching. Make two more clips ¼″ apart on either side of the corner clip for a total of five clips. Continue around the cording until you come back to the starting point. Cut away ½″ of cording inside the bias tube, lap the ending length over the beginning length ½″ or less, and end off.

Lay the piece of backing material on the needlepoint right sides facing. Pin the backing to the cording all the way around. Turn over so that the wrong side of the needlepoint is up. Machine-stitch the backing to the needlepoint on top of the hand stitching attaching the cording on three sides and all four corners, leaving a 8″ to 10″ opening on one side. Turn the pillow right side out. Stuff the pillow with polyester fiber, making sure to pack the corners well. Blind-stitch the opening closed by hand.

Do not add zippers to pillows—they are bulky, unsightly, and unnecessary. Most reputable dry cleaners will be able to clean the stuffed pillow without taking out the filling, as long as they know what the filling is. If you absolutely must remove the filling, the hand stitching closing up the fourth side can be removed easily and just as easily restitched after the pillow has been cleaned.

Another alternative is to make an inner pillow to hold the filling. Cut two pieces of cotton fabric (muslin is good) 1″ larger in each dimension than the finished needlepoint pillow will be. For instance, for a 16″-square pillow cut the material for the inner pillow into two 18″ squares. Stitch these together on three sides and four corners, with a ½″ seam. This will make the inner pillow 1″ larger than the needlepoint pillow and ensure that the needlepoint pillow will be firmly stuffed. Clip the corners and turn the inner pillow right side out. Press under a ½″ seam allowance on the open side, stuff, and close the fourth side with hand stitching, overcasting, or a narrow machine zigzag.

One disadvantage of using an inner pillow is that it doesn't provide as plump a stuffing for the corners of the finished pillow as does placing the filling directly into the needlepoint piece. This can be remedied by stuffing the corners of the needlepoint with extra filling after the inner pillow with the bulk of the filling has been inserted.

Suggestions for Other Uses

Any of the border designs from the rug can be used on articles made in strips, such as bellpulls, belts, drapery tie-backs, luggage-rack straps, bookmarks, headbands, chokers, guitar straps, suspenders, or hatbands.

On large-mesh canvas the main border with the two red borders on either side would look attractive on a director's chair. The same three borders, worked around a square or rectangle and leaving the center field open, would make a spectacular picture frame. One of the large medallions from the main border, surrounded by a band of the red-border design, would make a nice pincushion; or the medallion alone, worked on 12- or 10-mesh canvas, a coaster.

It goes without saying that the design would make a perfect needlepoint or cross-stitch rug. To work the Talish rug in the same manner that I worked the coverlet-pattern rug (figure 3-33)—that is, from selvedge to selvedge without any tedious finishing—I had to further adapt the design. I planned it for 40″-wide, 7-mesh Penelope canvas, with 250 meshes from selvedge to selvedge. The charted design for the pillow is 271 stitches square, so it was necessary to reduce the design by 22 stitches to measure 249 stitches. The extra mesh threads can be included as part of the selvedge and worked in binding stitch or split into two threads, one included in the outermost lengthwise row of light-blue cross-stitches, the other as part of the selvedge. The chart for making a needlepoint or cross-stitch rug based on the Talish rug is shown in figure 3-31.

Certain motifs and borders had to be moved or reduced in size, but these changes did not alter the basic character of the design. To work the design on 7-mesh canvas, use four plies of Persian yarn for cross-stitch; six plies for tent stitch. Follow the directions for making the coverlet-pattern rug—the next project in this chapter—and continue the borders to make as long a rug as you want. You will find in working the length that if you turn the corners after the

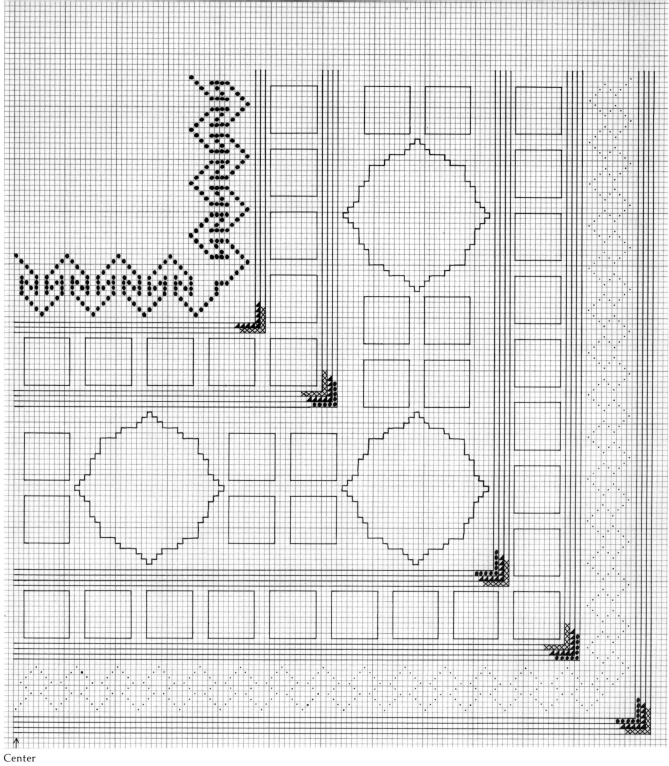

Center

3-31.

fourth, seventh, or tenth large medallion in the central border, the four corners of each separate border pattern will be alike, except one, and all four corners of the rug will be exactly the same. The pattern of reversing-arrowhead motifs in the central blue field will be the only area that is not perfectly symmetrical at the corners, but this is of little consequence, since it will be only one stitch off and can easily be made to look right. Most Caucasian rug makers did not worry about turning the corners perfectly.

WHIG ROSE COVERLET

While the beds of the wealthy in early America were sometimes adorned with elaborately embroidered hangings and spreads, beds in the average household were made up under woven coverlets (figure 3-32). These were made on handlooms, either by housewives or by professional weavers carrying on their trade as a cottage industry. Handwoven coverlets were undoubtedly made in the eighteenth century, although no dated examples survive. They were

3-32. Woven coverlet in the Single Snowball pattern, nineteenth century. (Author's collection. Photo by Ken Kaplowitz.)

72

certainly made in quantity in the first half of the nineteenth century. Many of the dated examples are from the 1830s and '40s. Their sturdy patterns go well with country furniture of many periods.

Coverlets adapt well to any form of counted-thread embroidery, since their design is also based on the geometrics of numbered threads. I based my chart on a coverlet pattern known as Whig Rose in the North and Methodist Wheel, or Ring, in the South. It is one of a number of patterns with interlocking wheels that would be effective translated into needle-work. For instance, the actual coverlet illustrated in figure 3-32 is in the Single Snowball pattern with the central motif solid rather than open.

I used blue and white, the most common color scheme for coverlets, although reds, browns, and sometimes greens are also found. Two projects, a rug and a pillow (figure 3-33), have been made up from the same chart so that you can see how very different effects can be produced from the same design through changes in scale, color relationships, and texture.

Cross-stitch Rug

The cross-stitch rug was done on 40"-wide canvas, 5 meshes per inch, and exactly 197 threads wide. The design was planned for this exact number of threads, so before you buy your canvas, count the threads while you are still in the store. This count does not include the selvedge edges, which are left bare until the main body of the rug is completed.

The rug is three circles plus borders wide by five circles plus borders long. For this size you will need 56" of canvas for the design area plus 4" for turnback. For a square rug three circles by three circles you will need 44" of canvas. For longer rugs figure your yardage by adding 9½" for each additional circle. Whatever size you choose, have your canvas cut a few inches more than is actually required just in case the mesh count in the length varies slightly.

For the 56" × 40" rug (unfringed measurement) you will need approximately 6½ pounds of Paterna Persian-wool yarn, of which 2 pounds should be white and the rest blue. The wool comes in 4-ounce skeins, which you should buy uncut. When you are working the rug, cut each skein through only once and use two long strands (six-ply) in the needle.

You should use a frame to stitch the rug—a project so large and cumbersome cannot be worked easily (or pleasurably) in the hand. Some frames are made of unfinished wood and are quite inexpensive; others are made of fine hardwoods, beautifully finished, and stand quite nicely in a living room or family room. You might even find that other members of your family are anxious to put in some stitches if they see the frame unoccupied with a threaded needle on hand.

3-33. Cross-stitch rug (40" × 60" excluding fringe) worked by the author and cross-stitch pillow worked by Lynda Pullen, both with a design adapted from a woven coverlet in the Whig Rose pattern. (Photo by Ken Kaplowitz.)

3-34.   Paterna Persian yarn numbers

☒ white 012   ☐ dark blue 365

To begin the rug, fold under 1½" to 2" of canvas so that the spaces between the canvas threads of the two layers match up and there are two horizontal canvas threads on the very edge. Baste this in place using carpet thread and Continental stitch over every other mesh.

If your rug frame does not have canvas or other fabric webbing attached to the two roller bars, staple or tack some on now. I have found that drapery pleater tape is very good for this purpose. Using the carpet thread double in the needle, overcast the canvas to the edge of the webbing through the last mesh opening on the turned-and-basted edge. Tack the far end of the canvas (the unbasted edge) directly to its roller bar—it will be basted back and sewn to its webbing later. Roll all of the canvas up on the far end so that you have a tightly stretched working area. Using either the hook devices that sometimes come with rug frames or heavy string, lace the selvedge edges tightly over the two sidepieces of the frame. When you are through, the canvas should have very little bounce.

You may, if you wish, count and mark the white part of the design from the chart (figure 3-34) directly onto the canvas using a pale-blue felt-tipped, oil-based marker as each unworked area is unrolled on the frame. This makes the stitching go much faster. Start working at the basted edge, stitching through the two layers of canvas as though they were one layer but leaving the two threads at the very edge free for knotting the fringe through when the rug is finished.

To begin and end each working thread (figure 3-35), weave through the double canvas threads that will be covered by each cross-stitch. Six to eight cross-stitches should cover the tag ends. Be sure to weave blue yarn into areas that will be covered by blue cross-stitches; white yarn, into areas covered by white cross-stitches. Running the yarn through the backs of completed stitches to start and end new threads would force you to keep turning the frame to enable you to see the wrong side. Weaving them through the canvas mesh is a much easier method and produces a much neater back.

Stitch the white areas of the design first, using cross-stitch and completing each stitch before moving on to the next. After the white areas are stitched, fill in the dark-blue areas. You may work the blue either by moving back and forth (figure 2-20), which is faster, or by completing each stitch separately (figure 2-19), which is slower but provides the best backing for the rug. It is easier to work the blue areas circle by circle rather than in long rows across the entire width.

As each area becomes filled with stitches, unlace the sides, roll up the worked areas and unroll blank canvas, relace the sides, mark the visible design area, and continue stitching. When the rug is as long as you want it to be—that is, when you have marked but not stitched the last border in the width—take the unworked end off the frame and baste back 1½" to 2" of the edge, just as with the first section of the rug, leaving two canvas threads on the very edge. Cut off any excess canvas, sew the basted edge to its webbing,

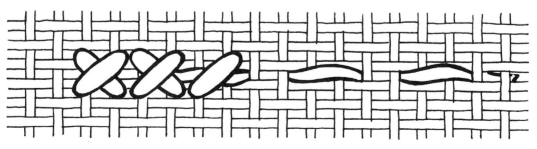

3-35.

and roll and lace tightly again. Mark your signature in one of the corners and finish stitching the rug.

Using the smaller alphabet in figure 2-49, graph out your signature and mark it on the canvas in one of the last two corners, remembering to face the lettering outward toward the edge. Use only two plies of yarn in your needle and cross-stitch the lettering over a single canvas-thread intersection rather than the two thread intersections used for the rest of the rug (figure 2-2).

Remove the entire rug from the frame and work binding stitch (figures 2-6, 2-7, and 2-8) over the two selvedge edges, moving forward four stitches and backward three stitches. For better coverage at the corners overcast ½" into the narrow width of the selvedge before working the binding stitch. You may have to use a pair of pliers to pull the needle and yarn through the selvedge or prepare a hole for each stitch with an icepick or awl.

To fringe the rug, cut 8" lengths of blue yarn by folding the long working lengths three times and cutting through the folds at each end. Using a crochet hook loop-knot two strands through each mesh over the two canvas threads at each short end. Since the rug was tightly laced and stretched on the frame while it was being worked and since cross-stitch distorts the canvas very little if at all, you will not have to block it. It will be ready for the floor as soon as the last piece of fringe is knotted in place.

You can paint or spray a nonskid backing on the wrong side to keep the rug from sliding on a bare floor. I do not recommend lining a needle-made rug, although many needleworkers do. Dirt and grit will be caught between the rug and the lining and may actually cut the yarn threads with prolonged use. Leaving the rug unlined allows the dirt to go through to the floor or pad below, where it can be easily cleaned up.

Cross-stitch Pillow

The cross-stitch pillow made by Lynda Pullen (figure 3-33) was done from the same chart as the cross-stitch rug (figure 3-34), but the colors were reversed. To make this pillow, buy cotton hardanger cloth (22 threads per inch, 11 cross-stitches per inch). The stitched design area on this fabric is 17¼". Have your fabric cut to a 22" square to allow for margins and seam allowances. Use two strands of D.M.C. six-strand cotton, color #336, or one strand of D.M.C. pearl cotton, size 8, in the same color. Stitch the design in cross-stitches over two fabric threads.

Work the design so that it forms a square— three circles plus border by three circles plus border. Do not mark the design on the fabric, as was done on the rug canvas, but stitch directly from the chart. After you have worked one motif of the border and one complete circle, you need only refer to your completed stitches to continue the design. Sign the pillow in a corner, following the same directions as for the rug. Work your cross-stitches for the signature half the size as those in the rest of the pillow, using one strand of the six-strand cotton.

To make the pillow, buy a package of bias cording or piping, matching the color to the color of the embroidery thread. Baste the cording to the front of the embroidery, folded edge on the embroidery, cut edge on the seam allowance. Stitch the cording to the embroidery by hand or machine, with the stitching line just a fraction of an inch outside the seam line in the seam allowance. At each corner clip the seam allowance of the cording just to the stitching, then ease the cording around the corner, making more clips if necessary. Continue around the pillow until you come back to the starting point. Cut away ½" of cording inside the bias tube, lap the ending length over the beginning length for no more than ½", and end off.

Cut a piece of backing material the size of the finished pillow plus at least ½" seam allowance. An unembroidered piece of hardanger cloth was used for the pillow shown here, but you can use a contrasting color if you prefer. Lay the piece of backing material on the embroidery, right sides facing. Pin the backing to the cording all the way around. Turn over so that the wrong side of the embroidered piece is up. Machine-stitch the backing to the embroidery, taking the machine stitches slightly inside the stitching that attaches the cording. Do this on three sides and all four corners, leaving an 8" to 10" opening on one side. Turn the pillow right side out.

Stuff the pillow with polyester fiber, making sure to pack the corners well. Blind-stitch the opening closed by hand. If you wish to use an inner pillow for the stuffing, see the directions in the Talish-pillow project.

Suggestions for Other Uses

The Whig Rose coverlet pattern would be useful for many square or rectangular articles. You may use the design in the white-on-blue or blue-on-white scheme or change the colors to suit your own decor.

Worked in needlepoint on 12-mesh canvas, this pattern would make a 16½" pillow. You could also work it in either needlepoint or cross-stitch to upholster a rectangular piano bench. In cross-stitch it would make a lovely long table or bureau runner.

In the same spirit as the original coverlet you could work the design in cross-stitch on 20-thread-count linen for a bedspread. Imagine how it would look with the cross-stitch rug on the floor at the foot of the bed!

FRAKTUR CERTIFICATE

Commemorating and recording important events has always been an important subject for craftsmanship. In needlework this has usually been done in the form of samplers, and you may find inspiration for celebrating a birth, marriage, or anniversary in antique examples.

For something a little out of the ordinary, however, I have turned to another source, the colorful illuminated manuscripts, called fraktur, painted by Pennsylvania Germans in the late eighteenth and early nineteenth centuries. These combined beautiful lettering in German Gothic alphabets with bright colors. Sometimes the illuminated letters themselves formed the chief design elements; at other times flowers, animals, birds, and human or angelic figures were added. Fraktur includes samples of calligraphy, religious sayings, certificates of confirmation, birth and baptismal certificates, marriage certificates, house blessings, and bookmarks.

Combining the Pennsylvania German tradition of drawn-and-painted documents and the colonial tradition of stitched samplers and family records, I have designed a family-record sampler for you to stitch

with a design taken from the 1841 Birth and Baptismal Certificate of Lewaina Bahr, who was born in Berks County, Pennsylvania in 1837. The manuscript was painted by Johannes Renninger in 1841. The original is in what is probably the greatest collection of fraktur in the country, the Borneman Collection of the Free Library of Philadelphia.

Fraktur Sampler

Choose a linen fabric with a high thread count to keep the completed size of the sampler manageable—say, a fabric with 32 threads per inch for a finished sampler, mounted on canvas stretchers, that measures 20" × 24".

To begin your sampler, first graph the lettering you wish to stitch. Use the larger alphabet in figure 2-49: it was the most common lettering form in antique samplers. Find the center of each row of lettering and mark it. Count the number of spaces on the widest line of lettering, multiply it by 2, and add 12. This figure gives you the minimum number of fabric threads needed in the width to accommodate the lettering of the widest line plus a six-thread margin on either side. Divide the number of threads per inch of your fabric into the figure just derived. This will give you the number of inches of fabric in the width that must be available for your lettering.

Enlarge the entire drawing (figure 3-36) by either the squares method in chapter 2 or by the photostat process so that the *inside*-width measurement of the large tablet enclosure is equal to the amount of fabric that must be available to accommodate the lettering. You should be able to accommodate at least 20 lines of lettering if necessary, leaving out the decorative motifs above and below.

In some cases, especially when there is a lot of lettering, it is preferable to stitch all the lettering before transferring the rest of the design to the fabric. After the lettering is stitched, the motifs surrounding the large tablet may be placed and transferred individually, which ensures that they will not crowd the tablet.

Weave a light sewing thread under two threads, then over two threads down the vertical center of the fabric. This guideline thread will help you to place your lettering and the rest of the design symmetri-

D.M.C. six-strand cotton
1 red 349
2 blue 312
3 green 367
4 yellow 743
5 brown 898 (also Belding Corticelli
silk buttonhole twist 5285)
6 black 310
7 flesh 945
8 snow white

3-36.

cally on the fabric. It is removed when all the stitching is done.

Put the enlarged drawing on tracing paper and transfer it to the fabric by any of the methods in chapter 2. Do not transfer any of the straight horizontal and vertical lines in the lettering-tablet enclosures. These are worked by following the threads of the fabric for crisper and more precise lines. In transferring the design pin the fabric down so that all the threads are as straight and taut as possible, keeping the pins well outside the design area.

Stitch the lettering in the large tablet first, using cross-stitch covering two threads and a single strand of buttonhole twist no more than 10″ long for each needleful. Center each line of lettering along the guideline thread. The rest of the sampler is stitched with six-strand cotton; experiment to see just how many strands are needed for each stitch area. You may use crewel wool, pearl cotton, or stranded silk if you prefer.

The large tablet is outlined in one line of stem stitch, except for three rows placed close together for the heavier outline around the double-arched bonnet. Follow a single fabric thread for each straight line of outlining. The red ovals in the bonnet and the blue point where the two arches meet are in satin stitch. The green and yellow squares down the sides of the tablet are in flat stitch, alternating the direction for each square. The bottom line of the enclosure is done in satin stitch. The twin semicircles at the top of the tablet are outlined in chain stitch. The "exclamation points" are done in satin stitch and outlined in stem stitch. Use French knots for the points. The horizontal lines are in stem stitch.

For the winged angel at the center top the face is done in brick stitch, and the features are overembroidered in stem stitch. The hair can be either long-and-short stitch or massed French knots. The inner part of the wings and the heart-shaped cloud on which the angel rests are in eyelet stitch, outlined in stem stitch. The outer wings are gold satin stitch, tipped in blue satin stitch, and striped in blue straight stitches. The large heart on the angel's breast and the crescent and small heart inside are all in satin stitch.

The dresses on the large angels on either side are in brick stitch overembroidered in straight single stitches (down the sides), double herringbone (along the hem), and open couching (under the hand). The remaining parts of the two angels, including the wings and sashes, are in satin stitch. The blue clouds upon which they stand are in long-and-short stitch. The wreath held by the angel on the right is done in lazy-daisy stitch. The bird held by the angel on the left is in satin stitch.

The flowerpot, birds, flowers, and leaves are done in satin stitch, with the decorative lines on the birds overembroidered in single black straight stitches. The flowerpot is outlined in stem stitch. Its yellow center is in satin stitch, with the direction of the stitches changed in every square to resemble woven basketry.

If, like Lynda Pullen, who made this sampler, you can trace your family way, way back, stitch the names and dates of the earliest members in the small boxes at either side of the top. If your family tree is short, stitch the words "FAMILY RECORD" in capital letters, one word in each box.

All of the stitches suggested here may be changed if you desire. The specified stitches are mostly flat and uncomplicated for a fairly untextured surface. Choosing other stitches will not only add more texture to the design but make the finished product more uniquely your own.

Suggestions for Other Uses

For a treasured gift to a newborn child the family-record sampler can be stitched for the same purpose as the original—that is, as a *Gebürts-und-Taufschein*, or birth-and-baptismal record. Nineteenth-century baptismal certificates were so highly treasured that they were sometimes buried with their owners.

The same design could be stitched as a *Trau-Schein*, or marriage certificate, or, with the addition of a prayer calling on God to save the house and all who pass through it from harm, a *Haus-Segen*, or house blessing.

The motifs in the design are simple enough so that, by enlarging and placing the design on a fairly high-mesh-count canvas, they could also be stitched in needlepoint.

TINWARE DOCUMENT BOX

Tinware has been called "poor man's silver." Its manufacture put into the average home useful and attractive articles that had once been available only to the rich in more valuable metals. Eighteenth-century tinware is comparatively rare and usually unpainted. Most of it was evidently imported from England. But by the first quarter of the nineteenth century the manufacture of tinware was well established in this country. By this time it was usually embellished with bold, brightly colored painting or stenciling.

When American antique tinware was first studied, most of it was attributed to the Pennsylvania Dutch, largely because the designs were somewhat similar to those found on their frakturs, barn signs, and pottery. Although a good deal was made in Pennsylvania, we know now that the major centers for the production of tinware were in New England, especially Connecticut and Maine. The fabled Yankee peddlers carried wares made in these centers throughout the states of the North, out to the new Midwest, and down South.

Although everything from kitchen utensils to lamps, toys, and presents for "tin anniversaries" was made from the metal, the most common forms seem to have been trays, coffeepots, and boxes. I based my designs for a place mat and a picture frame on one of the latter. It probably dates from the early part of the nineteenth century because of its original Hepplewhite brass handle. Probably made in New England, it has a delightful color scheme of yellow with touches of white on a Chinese-red background.

Place Mat and Picture Mat

The designs adapted from the front of the document box are simple to stitch. Only three basic stitches are used—stem, satin, and French knot—and two colors of size-8 D.M.C. pearl cotton—gold #742 and white blanc neige. Gloria Halpern made both the place mat and the picture mat, but the embroidery was done in the same way and in exactly the same size. They were both stitched on a brownish rusty-red polyester-and-cotton fabric called Kettlecloth. It is more difficult to embroider on synthetics or blends than on natural-fiber fabrics, but this fabric was chosen for this particular project because of its washability and durability.

To work the design for either the place mat or the picture mat, first enlarge the drawing (figure 3-37) to the required size by any of the methods described in chapter 2. The two samples were made to measure 14" × 16". At that size the center opening for the picture is 6" × 8". One yard of 45"-wide fabric will make and line two place mats or picture mats. Transfer the design to the fabric by any of the methods described in chapter 2.

The entire design is worked with gold thread except for the outlines and center veins of the curl shape in the outer border (shown as a heavier line in the drawing), which are worked in white stem stitch after the shapes are filled with satin stitch. The single straight line separating the inner and outer borders is done in stem stitch. The spiraling inner border is done in satin stitch, narrowing to stem stitch. The "exclamation points" are also done in satin stitch. The small circles are done in French knots with a single thread; the larger circles, French knots with two threads.

The shapes in both borders may be filled or not as you prefer—the drawing shows both. One suggestion is to use a woven filling in the outer border but not in the inner border. To make a woven filling, lay straight stitches, one thread width apart, across the shape to be filled, then cross those threads at right angles with straight stitches woven through the first stitches. The fillings for the inner border are long straight stitches or stem-stitch lines alternating with couched filling stitch and French knots.

There are many techniques for making place mats. The simplest would be to simply turn back the edges and hem them by hand or machine. I prefer adding a lining to embroidered place mats for added table protection and also to hide the wrong side of the work. To make a simple lined place mat, put the mat and lining right sides together, pin, then sew three sides together. Turn right side out, press, turn in the edges of the fourth side, and slip-stitch the opening closed by hand. A third method is to sandwich a layer of polyester batting between the lining and the embroidered top. Place the lining right side down, put the batting on top, and the embroidered mat on top

C-1. Bedspread (79" × 73½") from a set of bed hangings worked by Mary Bulman of York, Maine, c. 1745. (Courtesy of the Old Gaol Museum, York, Maine.)

C-2. Curtains made and worked by Bj Hensley with designs adapted from the Bulman bedspread shown in figure C-1. (Photo by Ken Kaplowitz.)

3-37.   D.M.C. pearl cotton, size 8
             gold 742
             white blanc neige

of that right side up. Baste close to the edges and diagonally across the mat from corner to corner. Enclose the edges in bias strips cut from the same or a contrasting material. You may add hand quilting to secure the batting if you wish. The sample place mat was made quite simply by sewing the embroidery to the lining along the two long sides, wrong sides facing. It was then turned right side out, pressed and a line of narrow zigzag stitches put in the two short sides directly on the seam line. The raw edges outside the lines of zigzag stitching were fringed by pulling out the fabric threads of both layers.

To finish the embroidery as a decorative mat for a picture, first cut a piece of heavy cardboard or mat board to the outside dimensions of the mat. Cut a hole in the center of the mat board the size of the picture. Use this cut board as a template and, on the wrong side of the embroidery, mark the opening, using a soft lead pencil. Do the same to a piece of facing fabric cut 2″ larger than the opening. Pin, then baste the facing piece to the right side of the embroidery, matching the marked openings. On the wrong side of the embroidery machine-sew the two pieces together along the marked lines, sewing with very small stitches (at least 20 to the inch) around the corners. If possible, stitch over the corners a second time. Cut away both layers of fabric inside the opening, leaving about 1″ around the edges. Make a slit through both layers of fabric into each corner, coming just up to but being careful not to accidentally clip the machine stitching. Lay the mat board on the wrong side of the embroidery and pull the facing through the center hole over the cardboard. Tape the facing temporarily in place. Bring the embroidery over the outer edges of the board and miter the corners, taping them temporarily in place. Using a very long length of heavy thread or string (I found size-3 pearl cotton excellent) and a sharp needle, lace back and forth between the facing and the embroidery around all four sides, pulling fairly tight and checking often on the right side to make sure that the embroidery is evenly aligned. Sew the mitered corners closed after the lacing is done.

If desired, a felt lining can be cut to the same measurements as the mat and glued to the back to hide the lacing; or a separate piece of matching fabric can be cut to the proper size, hems pressed back, and the lining slip-stitched to the back. Lay the picture over the opening, then lay a piece of cardboard cut to the same size as the picture over it. Tape the cardboard securely to the back of the mat and insert the beautifully matted picture into the frame of your choice.

Suggestions for Other Uses

The border designs from the box could be expanded to make a border for a tablecloth. The designs could also be used separately or together around the hems of skirts, sleeves, across shirt yokes, or as a border for shawls or curtains. The inner border could be used to stitch up beautiful embroidered suspenders or a belt. The entire design, worked as it was for the place mat, could be used to border a stitched motto or poem, which could then be made up into a pillow or a picture.

BLAZING STAR QUILT

No form of folk art is more typically American than the patchwork quilt. Quilting as a decorative device was certainly known elsewhere, but the idea of making beautiful utilitarian objects out of scraps of brightly colored cloth originated and was developed to its fullest extent in this country. Quilting was probably at its height in the nineteenth century, but the tradition has never died. In fact, it is now undergoing a revival, with quilters turning out both antique and modern designs.

The very names of many quilting patterns are evocative of the American experience—Log Cabin, Road to California, Courthouse Steps, Mariner's Compass, Bear's Paw. The variety of patterns in American quilts seems endless. Within this range certain motifs do appear and reappear frequently. Probably the most characteristic is the many-pointed star. Usually eight-pointed, the star could appear many times, or a single star could be expanded concentrically to cover the entire quilt, as in the Star of Bethlehem or Lone Star patterns.

The Blazing Star pattern that I have adapted was inspired by a quilt in which the patchwork stars alternate with appliquéd blocks (figure 3-38). Although quilts are usually associated with rural America, city cousins obviously made them as well. This

C-3. Bed rug worked in darning stitches by Elizabeth Foot in 1778. (Courtesy of the Connecticut Historical Society.)

C-4. Framed needlepoint worked by Susan Bailey with a design adapted from the Foot bed rug shown in figure C-3. (Photo by Ken Kaplowitz.)

C-5. Bargello purse in a carnation pattern, signed "George Gray, 1760." (Courtesy of the Philadelphia Museum of Art. Gift of Miss Helen Hamilton Robins.)

C-6. Bargello shoulder bag made and worked by Zelda Kaman with a design inspired by the Gray purse shown in figure C-5. (Photo by Ken Kaplowitz.)

one was stitched in 1845 by Amelia Sudlow, who lived at 127 West 16th Street in New York City. It is now in the hands of her direct descendants in what somehow seems a more appropriate setting, the still rural village of Hopewell, New Jersey.

Petit-point Picture

Patricia Kraus worked my adaptation of the Blazing Star quilt pattern on 18-mesh canvas with one strand of Persian yarn in the needle to form a framed picture 20″ square. Stitching on such fine canvas in such an intricate pattern produced a piece of needlepoint that from as close as 6′ away looks so much like real quilting that many experienced quilters and needle-pointers have had to come close and touch its surface to make sure that it really is needlepoint. The use of Scotch stitch in a muslinlike color for the background heightened the illusion.

The design area is 300 stitches square; each quarter of the graph is 150 stitches (figure 3-39). On 18-mesh canvas the complete design area is 16½″; on 14-mesh canvas, 21½″; on 12-mesh canvas, 25″; and on 10-mesh canvas, 30″. Whichever mesh of canvas you choose, be sure to include in your yardage at least 4″ for background and 4″ for unworked margin. Cut your canvas square and bind the edges to prevent them from raveling.

3-38. Pieced and appliquéd quilt in the Blazing Star pattern, made in 1845 by Amelia Elizabeth Sturges Sudlow. (Courtesy of Mr. and Mrs. Richard Sudlow. Photo by Ken Kaplowitz.)

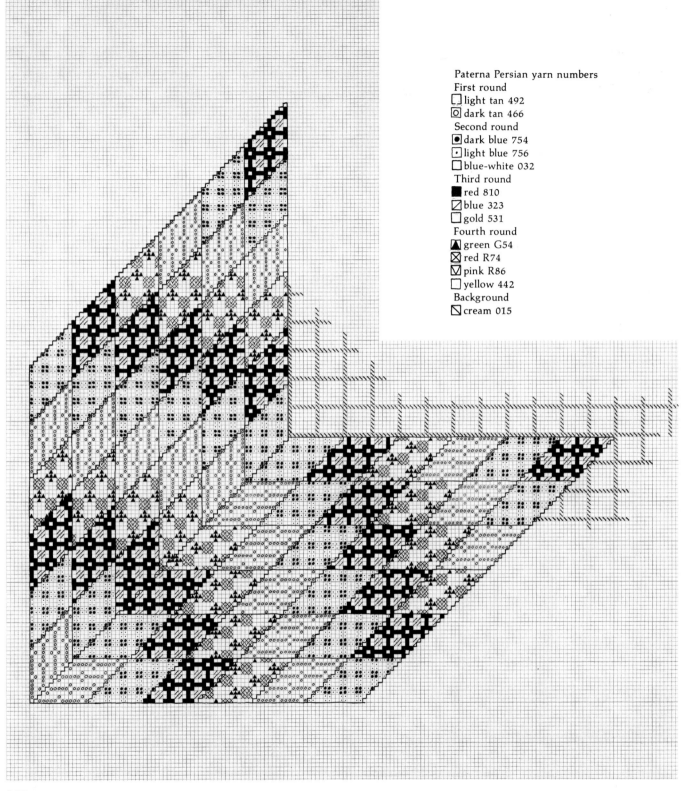

Paterna Persian yarn numbers
First round
☐ light tan 492
◉ dark tan 466
Second round
● dark blue 754
· light blue 756
☐ blue-white 032
Third round
■ red 810
▨ blue 323
☐ gold 531
Fourth round
◣ green G54
⊠ red R74
▽ pink R86
☐ yellow 442
Background
◪ cream 015

3-39.

C-7. Chinese Export polychrome plate, eighteenth century. (Courtesy of Pink House Antiques, New Hope, Pennsylvania. Photo by Allan Grow.)

C-8. Center of a needlepoint chair seat worked by Constance Greiff with a design inspired by the Chinese Export plate shown in figure C-7. (Photo by Ken Kaplowitz.)

C-9. Needlepoint pillow worked by the author with a design inspired by the Talish rug shown in figure 3-28. (Photo by Ken Kaplowitz.)

C-10. On the left a family-record sampler stitched by Lynda Pullen with a design inspired by the Birth and Baptismal Certificate of Lewaina Bahr, dated 1841, shown on the right. (Fraktur courtesy of the Rare Book Department, Free Library of Philadelphia. Photo by Ken Kaplowitz.)

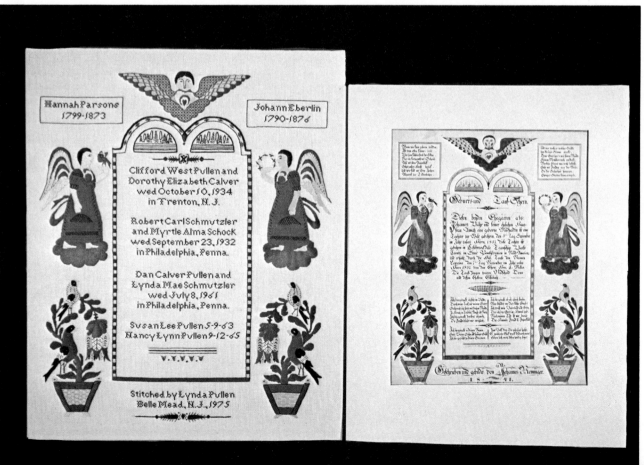

Fold the canvas in half twice to find the exact center. Notice that the design does not have one center stitch but four, one for each quadrant. To ease your stitching, with either markers or acrylics mark the outlines of each individual diamond shape onto the canvas-thread crossings, using the predominant color of each round—tan, blue, red, and yellow, for example. Stitch the design from the chart, turning the direction of your stitches each time you start a new quadrant so that the diagonal lines of each diamond are smooth, not jagged (figure 3-40). You will have to use the Continental stitch most of the time instead of the more desirable basket-weave stitch. If you work in the hand instead of on a frame, the canvas will get quite lumpy and bumpy, but do not despair! It will block out neat, smooth, and square.

If you wish to work the design on a larger mesh of canvas than the 18-mesh size, the design as charted may be much bigger than you want. You could adjust the size somewhat by making each individual diamond smaller. Our diamonds are 14 stitches long on the straight, 11 on the diagonal.

3-40.

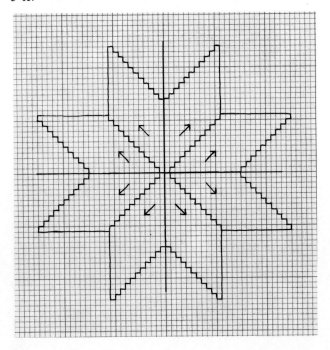

Deleting two rows (one on the straight, one on the diagonal) would make these lengths 13 and 10. Deleting more rows would leave less pattern in each diamond, and the effect of mixed printed-fabric scraps might be lost. Another way to make the design smaller would be to delete one entire round. Each large ray of the star would start to get smaller after the fifth round instead of after the sixth. The design could also be worked with each round of diamonds in a solid color in long satin stitches, stepped as in the chart, with the stitches turned so that they lie along the straight edge of each diamond (with the grain of the canvas). Stitched in this way, the design would work up very quickly, even on 16- or 18-mesh canvas.

After the design area is stitched, start filling in the background. Do not turn the direction of the background stitches, unlike the design stitches. Work the grid of tent stitches that surrounds the flat-stitch blocks first, making the first rows butt directly against the right angle in the center of one quadrant of the design. Space the lines of the grid so that flat stitches covering six canvas threads can be placed inside the small squares thus formed. Consistently continuing this pattern over the entire background will ensure that all four quadrants will be uniform.

If you are going to make the design into a pillow, add one more ply in your needle when filling in the squares to ensure adequate coverage and durability. If you are going to frame the design as a picture, work the background so that your finished piece will fit a standard-size artist's stretcher. Block the finished needlepoint following the directions in chapter 2. Directions for mounting the needlepoint on a stretcher are also supplied in chapter 2. I had a 20" frame made of unfinished pine with a decorative groove running along the length. It was very inexpensive and exactly right for the design. I could simply have had the molding cut to the proper size; joining the lengths at home to make the frame would have saved another one-third of the price. Have the framer measure the stretched needlepoint before making up the frame or cutting the molding. You may have put the stretcher together slightly off-square, which might necessitate adding ¼" to the size of the frame.

You have many choices in deciding how to finish your frame. One coat of clear wood sealer will protect the wood and leave it the natural color. You can stain the wood any color you wish and shellac or varnish it to give a soft or high gloss. I finished this frame with one coat of orange shellac covered by one coat of clear shellac. Paste wax can be put over any type of finish but should not be used on unsealed wood. To secure the stretched needlepoint in the frame, use either small finishing or wire nails, screws, and turn buttons; or screw eyes placed opposite each other in the frame and stretcher and wired together.

Suggestions for Other Uses

Worked solidly in cross-stitch on a countable-thread linen, the Blazing Star design would make a beautiful center for a square or round tablecloth. Deleting at least one full round of diamonds will make the design 250 stitches wide, just right to make a square rug on 40″-wide 7-mesh canvas. Any of the four small repeat patterns in the small diamonds may be taken out of the context of the quilt design and used as allover patterns on numerous small accessories—from wastebasket covers to neckties.

PAISLEY SHAWL

Only some of the elaborately patterned shawls known as Paisleys ought to be called by that name, for such shawls were woven in many places. Originally made in Kashmir in India, these fine woolen shawls were first imported to the West in the mid-eighteenth century. By 1800 they had become the height of fashion. Soon the British began to maufacture shawls based on Indian designs, first at Norwich and then at Edinburgh and Paisley in Scotland, from the latter of which the popular name comes.

Wherever the shawls were made, their designs were based on a pine cone with a curved tip. The cones were made up of garlands of flowers or, later, simply arabesques. The shawls were 6′ to 8′ squares or long rectangles, some reaching 12′. They came in many colors, but black and Turkey red predominated as grounds. After the Civil War, shawls gradually declined in popularity. Relegated to trunks and attics, they began to turn up in antique shops in this century. Until recently they were relatively inexpensive, but in the past few years prices have escalated. No matter what the cost, it seems almost sinful to cut up a Paisley to make a new garment, destroying an antique fabric. The owner of the skirt on which I based my design looked for over ten years before she found a shawl so ravaged by time and use that she could bear to cut it. It was a long rectangle, full of holes in the middle but with the wide side and end borders intact. It will take time and patience to work your own skirt based on the beautiful Paisley patterns, but not ten years! The skirt shown in figure 3-41 was embroidered and made by Janet Wyckoff in four months, with an interval for moving a family that includes two children and three St. Bernard dogs into a new house.

3-41. Detail showing the back of the embroidered skirt by Janet Wyckoff, adapted from a Paisley design. (Photo by Ken Kaplowitz.)

C-11. Embroidered place mat and picture frame, stitched by Gloria Halpern, both inspired by an early-nineteenth-century painted-tin document box. (Box courtesy of Ms. Valerie Cunningham. Photo by Ken Kaplowitz.)

C-12. Petit-point picture worked by Patricia Kraus with a design inspired by the Blazing Star quilt pattern shown in figure 3-38. (Photo by Ken Kaplowitz.)

C-13. On the left an embroidered evening skirt made and worked by Janet Wyckoff with a design inspired by the older skirt, made from a Paisley shawl, shown on the right. (Shawl courtesy of Constance Greiff. Photo by Ken Kaplowitz.)

C-14. Needlepoint for the top of a footstool, worked by Karen Potts with a tiger design taken from the *Godey's Lady's Book* of 1861. (Book courtesy of Mrs. Daniel Herrick. Photo by Ken Kaplowitz.)

Paisley Skirt

The fabric used for the skirt shown here is a black wool-and-polyester gabardine with the same weight and hand of the original shawl. The fabric you choose does not have to be black, as Kashmir and Paisley shawls can sometimes be found with red, green, blue, and even ivory backgrounds. Wash and dry (preshrink) your fabric before cutting the skirt pieces. Use D.M.C. pearl cotton for the embroidery to ensure continued washability even after the skirt is embroidered and made up.

The pattern for the skirt in the photograph had a 26½" waist, four seams, and a lower-hem circumference of 80¼". The pattern that you choose, no matter what size, should have about the same ratio between the waist and hem measurements. Cut out the four skirt pieces from the patterns and overcast the edges so they won't fray. Enlarge the front and back designs (figures 3-42 and 3-43) by the photostat process so that they fit inside the seam allowances of your pattern pieces. The skirt length can be modi-

Skirt front

Center front seam

3-42.

D.M.C. pearl cotton, size 5

1. dark red   815
2. bright red   321
3. blue   334
4. orange   740
5. white   blanc neige
6. black   310

Side seam

94

fied by continuing the repeating design motifs on either side of the center-front seam upward to the waist. Make two tracings of each enlarged design piece; the second tracing of each design should be the reverse of the first. Use a hot-iron-transfer pencil to redraw each tracing on the wrong side.

The only way to get the design onto the black fabric and still allow for changes while the work is in progress is to transfer the hot-iron-pencil drawing to a lightweight, loosely woven fabric such as muslin or organdy. Baste that onto the skirt fabric and embroider through both layers, pulling out the light fabric thread by thread with a pair of tweezers when the embroidery is completed (figure 3-44).

To start the skirt, sew the two front pieces together and the two back pieces together. Make sure that the designs match up on all seams. Embroider the fronts and the backs to within a few inches of the side seams, sew up the side seams, and complete the embroidery.

3-44. How to pull out the last bit of scrim after all the embroidery is finished. (Photo by Ken Kaplowitz.)

3-43.   Skirt back

Center back seam

Side seam

95

C-15. Wallpaper by William Morris, c. 1874–1876, called *Persian*. (Courtesy of the Cooper-Hewitt Museum.)

C-16. Needlepoint for a chair seat, worked by Patricia Wengel with a design inspired by the William Morris wallpaper shown in figure C-15. (Photo by Ken Kaplowitz.)

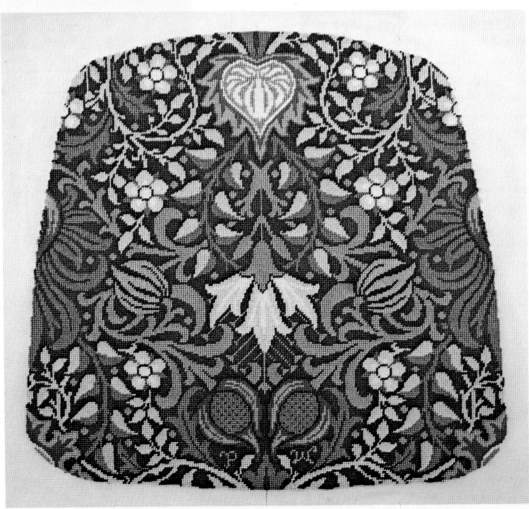

An embroidery hoop must be used to keep the two layers of fabric from shifting and to make sure that the stitching does not pucker the fabric. Since the finished embroidery must hang softly, keeping it smooth is very important. An oval hoop is best for working the skirt.

The designs shown here should not be taken as exact embroidery patterns. They are rather to be used as the basis for improvisations in the actual embroidery, each drawn line the inspiration for one, two, or even three lines of stitches, some in French knots, others in buttonhole, chain, or stem stitches. Areas to be lightly filled in with color should be done in couching, French knots, or Pekinese stitch. Other simple line and filling stitches can also be used. Much of the effectiveness of the embroidery lies in the lavish use of French knots—thousands upon thousands of them. I counted 200 in a 4″ square!

Although the black embroidery does not show up very much, it is very important for the texture it adds and for the exact spacing it provides for the parallel rows of stitching done in other colors on either side. If you can borrow or already have a Paisley shawl to study while you work your embroidery, you can match the placement of your colors to your particular shawl. If you cannot get hold of a shawl, just use your imagination and place the lines of color where you feel they look best. Your skirt can't help but turn out beautifully!

To make sure that you can wear your skirt for years and years (even if you put on a few pounds) and even pass it along someday to your daughter, do not put a zipper or darts in the skirt. Finish it by enclosing elastic in the simple folded waistband.

Embroidery of this magnitude and importance must be signed! You can add pockets in the side seams of the skirt and embroider your complete signature, date, and place in them. Your signature could also be placed on the inside of the waistband or hem.

Suggestions for Other Uses

The embroidery design for the back of the skirt can be used for the front as well: the back and the front will then be exactly the same. A beautiful caftan can be embroidered in this way, using the designs on either side of the center-front seam on the skirt as border designs on long, full sleeves.

A long, rectangular piece of the same type of material used to make the skirt or caftan could be made into a shawl or stole, embroidering the designs on the short sides. Instead of hemming the ends pull out some of the woven threads to make a self-fringe.

The design would also be spectacular for curtains or draperies in a room with Victorian furnishings.

GODEY'S LADY'S BOOK TIGER

A hundred years or more ago *Godey's Lady's Book* was *Vogue, Cosmopolitan, Ladies' Home Journal,* and *Ms* all rolled into one. *Godey's* printed fiction and poetry, campaigned for higher education for women, and instructed its readers in chemistry, as well as telling them how to cook, how to dress, how to behave, and how to decorate the home.

Each issue contained a "Work Department" and a section on embroidery. Occasionally, especially after midcentury, full-color charts were featured, such as the one from which I adapted the tiger in his jungle setting. It appeared as one of the frontispieces for the issue of January 1861. Although some of the beadwork and braiding illustrated are too elaborate for modern taste and some of the wonderful materials described can no longer be found, the *Lady's Book* is an almost endless source of authentic Victorian needlework designs.

Ten or fifteen years ago bound copies of a year's run of the *Lady's Book* could be picked up very reasonably in antique stores, but with revived interest in the nineteenth century prices have soared. Copies of *Godey's* or other magazines of the period can be found in many libraries, however, and you can probably run off a pattern on a copying machine or ask the librarian to have a photograph or photostat made for you. You may find, particularly with the color plates, that you will have to rechart the designs or use your imagination to compensate for the inadequacies of early color printing.

Pity the poor Victorian lady of 1861, trying to work her tiger design from the poorly printed color chart in the *Lady's Book*—the grid is uneven, the colors are blurred, and the shading is indistinct. My redrawing of the chart (figure 3-45), which indicates colors by color symbols, makes stitching this charming cat

3-45.

Paterna Persian yarn numbers

■	050 black	▯	504 darkest green
◉	424 darkest orange	⊠	520 dark green
⊠	434 dark orange	⊘	527 medium green
⊡	444 medium orange	⊞	542 light green
⊿	454 light orange	⊟	566 pale green
⊡	464 pale orange	▼	540 dark olive
◢	405 dark brown	⌊ᴸ⌋	553 medium olive
◣	410 medium brown	⊡	590 light olive
⊿	420 light brown	⒮	505 green
▽	430 pale brown	⊘	411 golden brown
		□	396 pale blue

much easier for today's needlepointer.

The design is 165 stitches wide by at least 110 stitches high. The height can vary because, since the sky is a solid color, it may be as high as you wish. Worked on 10-mesh canvas, it is still relatively small, although with 20 colors it is one of the more complicated designs in this book. You could make the design twice as large by working it entirely in cross-stitch over squares of four canvas threads.

Because the printing on the original chart read "top of stool," I thought it would be nice to do the same project over 100 years later. A very small Victorian Gothic Revival footstool or church kneeler was the inspiration. Richard Potts enlarged and simplified the design for a new footstool for his wife Karen Potts' needlepoint. Because the footstool was larger, the needlepoint was appliquéd to a piece of velvet, which formed a border around it and was used for the actual upholstery. The needlepoint will probably endure far longer than the velvet; when it is time for reupholstery, it can be removed from the old velvet, cleaned, and reappliquéd onto new velvet.

Tiger Footstool

Cut your canvas to the size required, leaving at least 2" of unworked-canvas margin on each side. Bind the cut edges of the canvas to prevent raveling. It is easiest to work the tiger first, starting with the black in the rear leg and tail, then working the orange colors from dark to light. When the tiger is stitched, fill in the ground and the jungle area. You can place your initials and the date inconspicuously in the lower-left-hand corner, using one of the darker greens used in the jungle. While much of the tiger, jungle, and ground have to be done in the Continental stitch, the sky can be worked totally in basket-weave stitch.

When the stitching is finished, block the needlepoint so that the corners form perfect 90° angles, following the directions supplied in chapter 2.

Appliquéing the Needlepoint to Other Fabric

Run two lines of machine-zigzag stitching, one on top of the other, 1" away from the worked area in the blank canvas.

Cut the excess canvas away close to the zigzag stitching, taking care not to cut the stitching.

Miter the corners first. With an ordinary lead pencil mark a diagonal line on the right side of the excess canvas, as shown by the marked threads in figure 3-46.

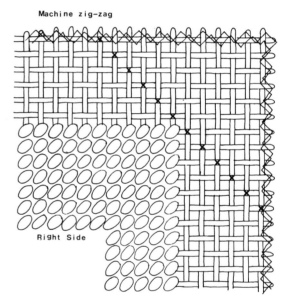

3-46.

Working with one corner at a time, fold the excess canvas at each corner back to the wrong side of the work along the marked line so that one end of the corner stitch is just visible from the wrong side (figure 3-47).

Make another fold in each corner, bringing the two halves of the marked line together over the back of the worked area. Whip the two marked lines together, using a sharp needle and heavy-duty sewing thread. Lay this whipped seam flat against the back of the worked piece.

Fold back the unworked sides and hand-hem them to the back of the needlework by sewing large, fairly loose overcasting stitches through the canvas threads that come out from the worked area rather than those that run parallel to it (figure 3-48). Try to pierce the canvas threads rather than sewing through the holes and make sure that your hemming stitches do not show on the right side.

Lay the mitered and hemmed needlepoint squarely on the fabric, making sure that you have left enough fabric for the upholstery. When you are sure that the needlepoint is properly positioned, baste it onto the fabric, taking fairly large stitches close to the edge.

To make sure that the appliquéing stitches do not pucker the fabric, pin the fabric to an open frame like a canvas stretcher. Do not stretch it too tightly, or you will make holes in the fabric. Stitch the needle-point to the fabric, using heavy-duty sewing thread, and place your stitches so that they lie invisibly between the stitches on the last row of needlepoint. Any large movements of the needle should be made under the fabric, not on the surface. Start the stitching at a corner and stitch all around, leaving the last 1" open—do not end off your thread.

To finish off the edge of the needlepoint and to hide the appliqué join, make a mock twisted cord as explained in the next paragraph and sew it down at the very edge of the needlepoint. For the cord use twelve full strands of needlepoint yarn, just as they come from the skein, cut through once. Sew the long strands together by machine, very close to the cut ends, using a straight stitch and sewing back and forth until they are secure.

Slip one of the stitched ends of the yarn bundle under the opening left between the needlepoint and the fabric. Twist the bundle towards the needlepoint once and, with a needle threaded with one long, full strand of matching yarn, whip this stitch twist through the edge of the needlepoint into the fabric. Bring the needle up quite close to where it went in. Twist the bundle again and whip the second twist down. Each twist should be ½" to ¾" long. Continue all around the needlepoint, making sure that the whipping stitch moves in the same direction as the twist so that it appears to be part of it. When you get

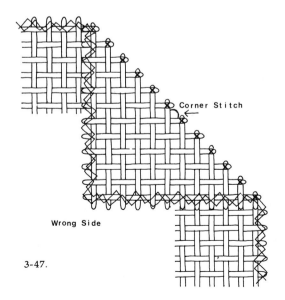

Corner Stitch

Wrong Side

3-47.

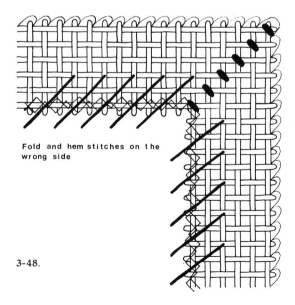

Fold and hem stitches on the wrong side

3-48.

100

back to the starting point, overlap the bundles by one twist and tuck in the ending length of the bundle just as you did in the beginning. Close up the opening, maneuvering your appliquéing needle under the twisted cord.

Upholstering the Footstool

Both footstools, the Victorian original and the 1975 adaptation, were very simply made—only four pieces of fine wood (walnut) for legs, four pieces for sides, and a piece of plywood for a platform top, which was screwed into the base. If you are having a stool made for your needlepoint, the top should be cut slightly smaller than the outside perimeter of the footstool, and the corners notched out or curved slightly to compensate for the thickness of the upholstery.

As you take the platform off the stool, mark the front of both with chalk so that they can be put back together correctly when the upholstering is done. Measure and mark with chalk the centers of all four sides of the fabric, stitched or woven, for the upholstery. Also mark the centers of the four sides of the platform top on the underside and on the sides.

Using a spray of liquid tape or any latex cement, glue a slab of 1" foam rubber to the top of the platform. Use an electric carving knife to cut the foam flush with the sides of the platform after it is glued on.

Put a layer of 1" cotton batting over the foam, bringing it down over the sides of the foam and the platform. Tear the batting to the proper size, using one hand as a straightedge to tear against.

Lay the fabric on top of the batting, matching the centers marked on the fabric and on the underside of the platform (figure 3-49). Using size-3 or -4 upholsterers' tacks, lightly tack the fabric centers to the platform. You may want to readjust the tacks, so don't hammer them all the way in. You may place temporary tacks on the sides of the platform but make sure not to pull the fabric so tightly that permanent holes will show. If desired, pushpins can be used for temporary tacking; staples in a staple gun, for permanent tacking.

Pull the fabric towards the corners and temporarily tack as close to the corners as possible. Don't pull the fabric too tightly, or you will compress the slight dome shape of the upholstery.

When you are sure that the placement is perfect, start putting in the permanent tacks, the front first, then the back, then the sides. Start at the center of each side and work out to the edges, pulling the excess material out to the corners. Tack to within 2" of the corners, placing the tacks ¾" to 1" apart so that pull marks do not show on the top.

The pleats that neatly fold away the excess fabric at the corners will actually be placed on the front and back of the platform so that the fold openings can only be seen from the sides. Smoothing the excess fabric down from the top towards the corners along the grain of the fabric, pull the excess from the side around to the front and tack it on the edge of the front (figure 3-50). This tack will be covered by the rest of the pleat.

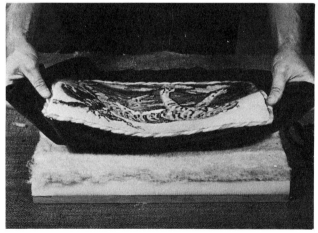

3-49.

3-50.

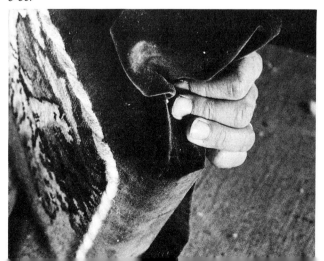

Cut off the excess fabric in the folded underside of the pleat on the straight of the fabric, not on the diagonal or the bias. The cuts are made so that the corners will not be too bulky when the pleat is finally folded and tacked. Fold the pleat slightly short of the corner and pull it to the corner for a sharp edge (figure 3-51). Use a nail file to push in the fold of the pleat and to keep the edges sharp and straight. Press the fold flat by lightly tapping it with a hammer. Tack the pleated corner on the underside of the platform, placing the tacks ¼" apart. After the pleat is folded and tacked, the fold opening can be sewn closed invisibly with a curved needle and light thread.

Cut 1½" lengthwise or bias strips of the fabric for cording. Using matching thread, join the strips with bias seams by machine—butt joins don't hold as well. If you are using velvet, make sure that the pile or nap will lie in the same direction after the strips are joined. Keeping the joining seams open, make cording from the long strip with the cording foot on your machine (figure 3-52).

Put the cording on the underside of the platform so that it lies flush to the edge and tack it in place (figure 3-53). Notch the inner edge of the cording as it moves around the corners of the platform. To join the two ends of the cording, open the first edge and cut out about ½" to 1" of the filler. Lap the ending length into the beginning. Fold the open end under a little to prevent the cut edge from fraying.

To finish the underside neatly, cut a piece of muslin or cambric to the size of the platform plus 1". Fold it under 1" on all four sides and tack it in place.

If the platform is held in position by pegs in the stool that fit into holes in the platform, punch holes through the pieces of fabric into the holes and reinforce the fabric holes with a few extra tacks. Fit the upholstered platform on the footstool, sit down in a comfortable chair, and put your feet up (figure 3-54).

Suggestions for Other Uses

The tiger design can be framed as a picture and hung on the wall. Stitched and appliquéd to velvet in the same way as for the footstool, the design could be made up into a pillow, using the same velvet for backing. A tasseled silk fringe instead of cording would make it extremely luxurious!

3-51.

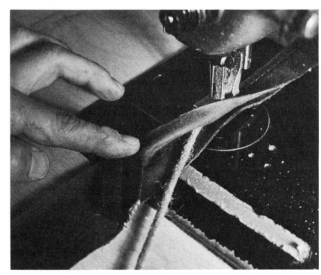

3-52.

3-53.

The tiger itself could be lifted from the background and stitched on a piece of clothing, such as the back yoke of a blue-jean jacket. To do this, baste a piece of fairly high-mesh-count cross-stitch canvas to the fabric and work the design through both layers, in either needlepoint or cross-stitch, being careful not to pierce the canvas threads. When all the stitching is complete, pull out the canvas threads with a pair of tweezers. The design will be permanently stitched onto the fabric.

3-54.

WILLIAM MORRIS WALLPAPER

In the third quarter of the nineteenth century popular taste seemed to become increasingly flamboyant and extravagant. At the same time a number of reformers were preaching the gospel of simplicity and a return to fine craftsmanship. In the vanguard of reform was William Morris. After graduating from Oxford University he formed Morris and Company in 1861 with Edward Burne-Jones, architect Philip Webb, and others. Influenced by the writings of John Ruskin, the group turned back to medieval sources for inspiration, to the village crafts of "Merrie Olde England." Although their appreciation for the craftsmanship of the past was genuine, it was tinged by romanticism, and much of their work has a prettiness that is far removed from the spirit of the Middle Ages.

Morris and Company first produced stained glass, furniture, and embroideries. They soon expanded into the design and production of wall papers and fabrics, and it was through these that Morris' work became most widely known. Many of the chintzes and wallpapers have been in continuous production since they were first designed. Their naturalistic forms, abstracted somewhat into beautiful curves, and marvelous color sense have a universal appeal well calculated to withstand the test of time.

The wallpaper on which I based my design for a chair seat is called *Persian*. It was first made between 1874 and 1876 and reissued in the 1920s. It is typical of Morris designs that influenced interior decoration not only in England but in the United States as well. For all his rebellion against the popular taste of his own era, Morris' designs appear to modern eyes very much the product of the late nineteenth century. They both recall the Second Empire fashions of the late 1850s and '60s and look forward to the looser, more voluptuous curves of art nouveau, providing a pleasing complement to the style of much nineteenth-century furniture. *Persian* is a rather large, repeating design, suitable for upholstering many different kinds of furniture besides the chair illustrated here.

William Morris Chair Seat

Before preparing your canvas you must make a pattern so that the needlepoint actually fits the chair that it is being made for. The pattern is also used as a guide for blocking the finished needlepoint. If your chair is the kind in which the upholstered seat lifts out from the wooden frame of the chair by means of a screw or pegs—called a slip seat—remove the seat before making your pattern. If your chair does not need reupholstery but just a new covering, it may be possible to remove the old fabric carefully and use it as the pattern for your needlepoint. If your chair is to be reupholstered or if removing the old fabric is impossible, you will have to make a cloth pattern yourself. To do this, use muslin or an old sheet. Lay it on the seat and pin it all around the edges, making soft, even pleats in the corners where it drops down the sides. Cut off the excess fabric where the chair back, arms, and legs change the regular shape of the seat. Take the cloth pattern off the chair, fold it in half from front to back, and press along the fold. Check the folded pattern to make sure that the two sides are exactly the same and mark the exact center.

The canvas that you work on should be rectangular, no matter what the shape of the seat, and at least 4" larger than the pattern in each direction. Bind the edges of the canvas with masking tape to prevent them from raveling. Lay the folded cloth pattern on the canvas, making sure to place the fold along a single canvas thread running from top to bottom. Mark this center thread. Open out the fold and pin the entire cloth pattern to the canvas. Then mark the outline of the pattern onto the canvas, 1" beyond all the way around.

How much of the design will show depends on the size of the article to be upholstered and the mesh of the canvas on which it is worked. The design is so busy and colorful that a full repeat is not necessary. The slip-seat chair that Pat Wengel covered does not show the entire design (a full repeat), even though it was worked on 14-mesh canvas.

The design repeats vertically every 232 stitches. This repeat is quite apparent in the chart (figure 3-55).

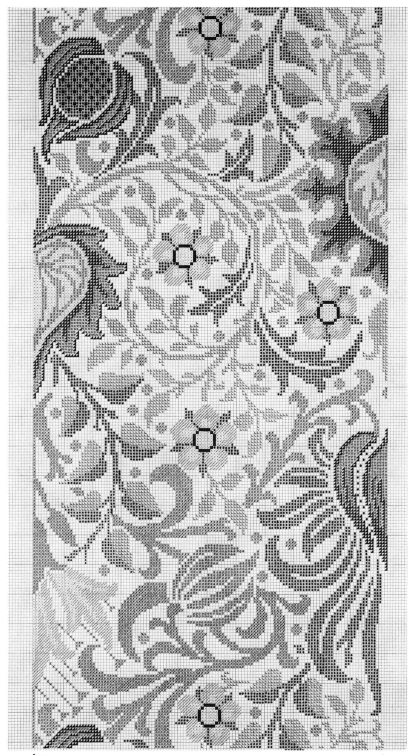

3-55.

Two color schemes

Paterna Persian yarn numbers

◩	wine red 231	orange 424
⊙	pink 282	pale orange 444
◪	gold 453	tan 466
·	white 040	white 020
◪	yellow 442	yellow 437
⌊	light green 566	light blue-green 556
⊠	medium green 542	medium blue-green 546
⊙	dark green 527	dark blue-green 522
■ □	background 504	background 340

↑ Center
do not repeat this vertical row

↑ Center
do not repeat this vertical row

A full horizontal repeat occurs every 246 stitches, although the chart shows only 124 stitches, or one-half of the design plus the center row. This is because the design repeats back on itself from both the left and the right side. To work the design, first draw a line down the exact center thread of the canvas. Follow the design from the chart, reading it from left to right and stitching over the centerline to the right side. When the right-hand limit of the chart is reached, some design areas will remain to be stitched on the right-hand side of the canvas. Do not repeat the last vertical row of stitches: start reading the chart backwards from the right side to the left side—that is, in mirror image—until you again reach the left side of the chart. Complete the left-hand side of the canvas by reading the chart in mirror image, stitching from left to right (do not repeat the row that covers the centerline on the canvas), then back again from right to left as charted.

Because reading and stitching from the chart in mirror image can be very confusing, you can have the chart enlarged by the photostat process so that the grid measures 10 squares to the inch. Trace the outline of each color area onto tracing-weight graph paper that is also printed with a 10-per-inch grid (available in art-supply stores). You can then stitch from both sides of the tracing-paper chart—the reverse side, which will be easy to read, is the mirror image.

In stitching from the chart outline each separate color area with Continental stitch, then fill in the areas with basket-weave stitch. This keeps your work from being distorted and makes it more portable—you don't have to carry your chart around at all times.

Stitched on 10-mesh canvas, the design would need 23½" vertically and 24½" horizontally to show a complete repeat. On 12-mesh canvas the design would need 19½" vertically and 20½" horizontally; on 14-mesh canvas, 16½" vertically and 17½" horizontally.

In planning your own needlepoint you may place any of the motifs on either side of the chart along the vertical centerline of the canvas. Just remember that the last vertical rows on the left- and right-hand sides of the chart are not repeated when the design starts doubling back.

Two different color combinations are suggested here. The oranges and blue-greens of the contemporary piece were chosen by Pat Wengel to complement the decor of the room in which the chair was placed. Although the chair is from the early nineteenth century and the upholstery design from the late nineteenth century, they suit each other. Pinks and true greens, an alternate combination, are closer to the colors of the original wallpaper.

Recovering an Antique Slip-seat Chair

If you remove the old covering on an antique chair, you may find that some of the tacks have been driven below the surface of the wood. Do not try to remove those tacks: this would chew up the old, dry wood even more. Just leave them where they are and work around them.

If the covering on the slip seat is fairly thin and the seat is the type that drops into the wooden frame of the chair without being held by screws or pegs, test the seat with the needlepoint on top to see if it will fit back into the frame with the thicker covering. If you have to force the seat back into the chair, you may eventually split some of the glued joints. If the fit is too tight, it is better to pull up the muslin covering the old webbed upholstery on the seat and plane off some of the wood frame. Do not make adjustments on the chair itself.

To eliminate some of the sag in the center of the seat without reupholstering the entire seat, put one layer of 1" cotton batting right in the center and cover the entire top with another layer, making sure that you do not lap any of the batting over the sides of the seat (figure 3-56). Tear the batting to size—do not cut it.

Measure and lightly mark the center of all four sides of the needlepoint and the seat frame with a piece of chalk.

Using size-3 or -4 upholsterers' tacks, temporarily tack the needlepoint to the front and back of the frame, matching the marked centers. If the wood is very old and full of tack holes, you may want to use size-5 or -6 tacks for better hold. Pushpins can be used for temporary tacking; staples in a staple gun, for permanent tacking. It is all right to tack through the blank-canvas margins, but for greater strength it is better to tack through the stitched needlepoint.

Pull the sides of the needlepoint down and tack them temporarily in the corresponding frame centers. Check continually to see that you have pulled evenly on all sides and that the design is still placed correctly.

When you are sure that the placement is perfect, start putting in the permanent tacks, doing the front first, then the back, then the sides. Start at the center of each side and work out to the edges, pulling the excess material to the corners. Tack to within 2″ of the corners, placing the tacks ¾″ to 1″ apart so that pull marks do not show on the top (figure 3-57).

The pleats that are made to fold away the excess needlepoint on the corners are actually placed on the front and back of the seat so that the fold openings can only be seen from the sides. Smoothing the excess from the top down towards the corners along the grain of the needlepoint, pull it from the side around to the front and tack it on the front edge. This tack will be covered by the rest of the pleat.

Cut off the excess in the folded underside of the pleat on the straight of the needlepoint, not on the diagonal or the bias (figure 3-58). The cuts are made so that the corners will not be too bulky when the pleat is finally folded and tacked. Fold the pleat slightly short of the corner and pull it to the corner for a sharp edge (figure 3-59). Use a nail file to push in the fold of the pleat and to keep the edges sharp and straight. Press the fold flat by lightly tapping it with a hammer. Tack the pleated corner on the underside, placing the tacks ¼″ apart. After the pleat is folded and tacked, the fold opening can be sewn closed invisibly with a curved needle and light thread.

3-57.

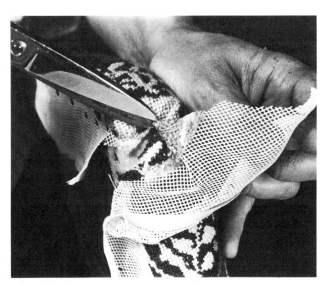

3-58.

3-59.

3-56.

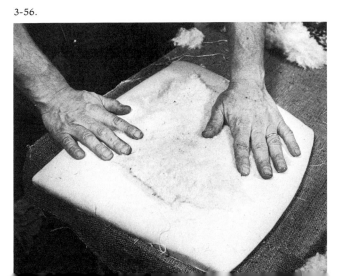

To finish the underside neatly, cut muslin or cambric to the size of the seat plus 1". Fold under 1" on all four sides and tack it in place. The finished chair seat is shown in figure 3-60.

3-60.

Suggestions for Other Uses

Worked on 14- or even 18-mesh canvas, the William Morris wallpaper design would make a beautiful vest or bolero for either a man or a woman. Buy a pattern in the proper size. Since needlepoint is rather stiff, be sure that the pattern is properly adjusted by making the vest up in another fabric first. Lay the pattern pieces under the canvas and trace all markings onto it. Be sure to mark the seam line and darts carefully. Do not cut the canvas into the pattern shape until all stitching is done. Plan to place half of one of the major motifs on either side of the front opening and the same motif on the center back.

To eliminate excess bulk, do not stitch in the seam allowances or the darts. When the needlepoint is complete, block all pieces to match the pattern. Cut off all excess canvas to within 1″ of the needlepoint and run machine-zigzag stitching over the cut edge. Run a line of straight machine stitching around all pieces at the very edge of the needlepoint. You may follow the pattern directions for making up the vest or bolero, but much of the work should be done by hand. Be sure to slash the canvas seam allowances only to the line of straight machine stitching in working around curves. Instead of just pressing them open, canvas seam allowances should be sewn to either the facings, interfacings, or back of the needlepoint (according to the provisions of your pattern) to ensure smooth, unbulky edges.

INDEX